Living on the Surface

LIVING ON
THE SURFACE

New and Selected Poems by

MILLER WILLIAMS

Louisiana State University Press
Baton Rouge and London
1989

Copyright © 1972, 1975, 1976, 1979, 1980, 1982, 1987, 1988, 1989 by Miller
  Williams
All rights reserved
Manufactured in the United States of America

98 97   5 4 3 2

Designer: Albert Crochet
Typeface: Linotron Palatino
Typesetter: G & S Typesetters, Inc.
Printer and Binder: Thomson-Shore, Inc.
LIBRARY OF CONGRESS CATALOGING-IN-PUBLICATION DATA

Williams, Miller.
  Living on the surface : new and selected poems / by Miller
Williams.
      p.   cm.
  ISBN 0-8071-1573-8. — ISBN 0-8071-1574-6 (pbk.)
  I. Title.
  PS3545.I53352L58   1989
  811'.54—dc20   89-33078
                                                           CIP

The books from which the poems herein have been selected are: *A Circle of
Stone* (Baton Rouge, 1964), copyright © 1964 by Louisiana State University
Press; *So Long at the Fair* (New York, 1968), copyright © 1968, 1967, 1966, 1965,
1964, 1963, 1960, 1958 by Miller Williams; *The Only World There Is* (New York,
1971), copyright © 1971, 1970, 1969, 1968 by Miller Williams; *Halfway from Hoxie*
(Baton Rouge, 1973), copyright © 1964, 1968, 1971, 1973 by Miller Williams;
Why God Permits Evil (Baton Rouge, 1977), copyright © 1977 by Miller Williams;
Distractions (Baton Rouge, 1981), copyright © 1981 by Miller Williams; *The Boys
on Their Bony Mules* (Baton Rouge, 1983), copyright © 1983 by Miller Williams;
and *Imperfect Love* (Baton Rouge, 1986), copyright © 1983, 1984, 1985, 1986 by
Miller Williams. Thanks are offered to the editors of the following publications,
in which some of the poems in this volume previously appeared, a few in
different versions: *The American Poetry Review, The American Scholar, Antioch
Review, Arkansas Times, The Barataria Review, Bits, Black Box, Boulevard, Brown
Paper Bag, Chariton Review, Chicago Review, Cimarron Review, Concerning Poetry,
Cornfield Review, Denver Quarterly, The Dickinson Review, Epos, The Falcon, Georgia
Review, The Ghent Quarterly, Jeopardy, The Kenyon Review, Light Year, The
Mediterranean Review, Missouri Review, Motive, MSS, Negative Capability, New
England Review, New Orleans Review, Ohio Journal, The Pan American Review,
Ploughshares, Poetry, Poetry Northwest, Poetry Now, Prairie Schooner, Red Weather,
Saturday Review, Southern Poetry Review, Three Penny Review, Three Rivers Poetry
Review,* and *Yankee.* "On the Death of a Middle-Aged Man" is reprinted from
Genesis West 6. "For Lucy, on Her Birthday" was originally published in *Nimrod*
(Spring, 1958). "Voice of America" first appeared in *December*, XII. "Reading the
Newspaper on Microfilm" and "Why God Permits Evil: For Answer to This
Question of Interest to Many Write Bible Answers Dept. E–7" first appeared
in *The Southern Review.*

The paper in this book meets the guidelines for permanence and durability of
the Committee on Production Guidelines for Book Longevity of the Council on
Library Resources. ∞

For Jordan

Contents

From *The Boys on Their Bony Mules* **(1983)**

From *Imperfect Love* (1986)

New Poems

Living on the Surface

The Associate Professor Delivers an
Exhortation to His Failing Students

Now when the frogs
that gave their lives for nothing
are washed from the brains and pans
we laid them in
I leave to you
who most excusably misunderstand
the margins of my talks
which because I am wise
and am a coward
were not appended to the syllabus

but I will fail to tell you
what I tell you
even before you fail to understand
so we might
in a manner of speaking
go down together.

I should have told you something of importance
to give at least a meaning
to the letter:

how, after hope, it sometimes happens

a girl, anonymous as beer,
telling forgotten things in a cheap bar

how she could have taught here as well as I.
Better.

The day I talked about the conduction of currents
I meant to say
be careful about getting hung up in the brain's things
that send you screaming like madmen through the town
or make you
like the man in front of the Safeway store
that preaches on Saturday afternoons
a clown.

The day I lectured on adrenalin
I meant to tell you
as you were coming down
slowly out of the hills of certainty
empty your mind of the hopes that held you there.
Make a catechism of all your fears

and say it over:

this is the most of you . . . who knows . . . the best
where God was born
and heaven and confession
and half of love

From the fear of falling
and being flushed away
to the gulp of the suckhole and that rusting gut
from which no Jonah comes

that there is no Jesus and no hell

that God
square root of something equal to all
will not feel the imbalance when you fall

that rotting you will lie unbelievably alone
to be sucked up by some insignificant oak
as a child draws milk through straws
to be his bone.

These are the gravity that holds us together
toward our common sun

every hope getting out of hand
slings us hopelessly outward one by one
till all that kept us common is undone.

The day you took the test
I would have told you this:
that you had no time to listen for questions
hunting out the answers in your files
is surely the kind of irony
poems are made of

that all the answers at best are less than half

and you would have remembered
Lazarus
who hung around with God or the devil for days
and nobody asked him

anything

But if they do
If one Sunday morning they should ask you
the only thing that matters after all
tell them the only thing you know is true

tell them failing is an act of love
because
like sin
it is the commonality within

how failing together we shall finally pass
how to pomp and circumstance all of a class
noble of eye, blind mares between our knees,
lances ready, we ride to Hercules.

The day I said this had I meant to hope
some impossible punk on a cold slope
stupidly alone
would build himself a fire
to make of me an idiot

and a liar

The Woman on the Porch

You would have said
if you could have seen her there
skin of a cow's udder hung beneath her eyes

you would have said
your loveliness is lost

left in paper bags beside your husband
black with pigs' blood and the waters of your children

you move your lips as if they have lost one another
touching and touching
like blind ants coming together

you make the sound breathing
you would say
of rats running.

If you had gone back to the gate
holding her there in your eyes
and that house

the chair she rocked in and the shoes coming clump
to the floor

if you could have known
if it had come to you
what she was doing
that she was all the rocking around the earth
that she drove rocking all the back and forth
up down and open shut all came from here
that she was every breathing and fish gill
rope skip run go in and out the window

spring and ratchet for every come and go
swing me high let the cat die
prayer wheeling prince
do it fast and fistly
rock-tock for all the trot a horse
and woah

hardtit twelve and lover housewife and whore
go together backseat bed and floor.

From here funeral home fans
moved the air in buzzing Sunday heat
swept flies from faces closed on sleep
and kept communion
between the sermon and the falling thoughts.

If knowing as I did she knew
she had looked at you
changing her face to knowledge I could not stand
would you not have killed her

if you had seen her on the deceiving porch
of ordinary wood crawled through by weeds

rocking only as fast as I could breathe?

(there are spiders who spin your name
if you tell a lie
and when they finish the letters
you have to die)

Because there is truth not to be believed
or if known denied
I did it
before the nibbling lips had split
to the turned-in toothless grin of recognition

(the sea sinks after ships that drown
to make a mouth the boats are swallowed down)

And a hand more thin than a bird's wing motioned me in
offered the empty bladder of her bust
and a place where knowledge was and forgotten vision
pulled at me like whirlpools and god's lust.

On the Death of a Middle-Aged Man

Beverly
who wished his mother wanting a girl again
had called him something at best ambiguous
like Francis or Marion
went for fifteen years to the Packard plant
and turned for Helen who punched the proper holes
bumperless bodies.

He took her
to dinner once and left her notes in secret
when hair fell down to his forehead and refused
the foreman's job.

Except for
when she was seven her brother which couldn't count
when she was twelve the preacher and that was for God
she never did nothing

Christ would have died for.
Going home
before the coffin was lowered because of the clouds
he fell in front of a car because of the rain.
There were just enough
to bear him
counting the foreman a man from the shift a cousin
come to lay claim.

A woman played the piano.
A minister who kept forgetting his name
said he was forgiven
that he would be forever
at the bosom of Abraham
which was the preacher's way of saying heaven.

For Lucy, on Her Birthday

Were you born as I was, beautiful witch?

I think you were spun by spiders
on a black mountain.

How woman were you I took as only woman.
Then there was magic, and before I knew
you were wind and dust and summer days
rain across the window
cold and holy water

and white fire.

What can I bring, extraordinary woman?
Wings of bats

or moon dark?

Original Sin

Wednesday nights
I walked in shadows past prayer meeting lights
and gave my time
for an hour and a half at the movies
and god's dime.

I was scared
when the girl who sold the tickets because she was dared
by a man as old
as my father let me feel.
She was cold

and this surprise
was my revelation—but I made lies
and looking at her
twisted my mouth as if it
didn't matter.

In bed my hand
was cold still and the fingers I let pretend
that she was lying
white on a blue hill,
birds flying.

Slowly wrong
I love my wife a time and the night long
I feel the hair
of a high girl grinning red
a night of prayer.

The Caterpillar

Today on the lip of a bowl in the backyard
we watched a caterpillar caught in the circle
of his larval assumptions

My daughter counted
half a dozen times he went around
before rolling back and laughing
I'm a caterpillar, look
she left him
measuring out his slow green way to some place
there must have been a picture of inside him

After supper
coming from putting the car up
we stopped to look
figured he crossed the yard
once every hour
and left him
when we went to bed
wrinkling no closer to my landlord's leaves
than when he somehow fell to his private circle

Later I followed
barefeet and doorclicks of my daughter
to the yard   the bowl
a milkwhite moonlight eye
in the black grass

It died

I said honey they don't live very long

In bed again
re-covered and re-kissed
she locked her arms and mumbling love to mine
until turning she slipped
into the deep bone-bottomed dish
of sleep

Stumbling drunk around the rim
I hold
the words she said to me across the dark

*I think he thought he was
going in a straight line*

9

And When in Scenes of Glory

When I had been born eight years I was born again
washed in the waters of life
and saved from hell
from the devil the Baptists the Campbellites
and the Pope

When I was told about Santa Claus and the sun
and learned for myself
that trees feel their leaves fall off
and scream at night

I thought about Jesus Christ who had long hair
was hung by the hands
buried and came alive

(in the Roxy Saturday afternoons
rag-dragging zombies came alive in caves
the blood of people made them live forever)

God come down

With hands that could have torn the hills apart
the preacher hammered the tinfoil of my faith
and words came teaching me
out of the terrible whirlwind of his mouth
the taste of evil
bitter and hot as belch
the agony of God
building the gospel word by believable word
out of the wooden syllables of the South

God come down

and over the pews over the dry domes
amens rose up like birds
beating the air for heaven
heading for home and roost
in the right eye

come for the sake of Jesus

and the white thigh
of Mrs. Someone sitting in the choir

boy do you believe

Yes Sir I do

A woman so skinny I could smell her bones
hugged me because I'd turned away from sin

Going home at night after the preaching
after prayers and dinner on the ground
curling in the backseat of the car
I began to feel like a thickening of the dark
almost my mother talking to my father
almost my father singing to himself
my name a gospel song
and a long applause like gravel under the tires

until I heard the wings
and knew it had come
what I had killed and couldn't come anymore
to hunger against the black glass of the car
the thing you think what would happen
if you saw its face

I'd have prayed to God not to have a flat
but God would have laughed
and it would have sounded like
the flapping of wings
over the old Dodge
over the grinding of gravel
and the hymn of grace

Floating with fishes under the river of sound
I remembered with my last dull thought
before I drowned
that I was saved from sin and the world was lost

The river stopped
and the world stopped
and I am lifted up

to be dropped again by my father
onto an unmade bed in a borrowed room
to wait my ankles crossed holding my breath
a dumb kid in some silly game
for the law straining around the earth to crack
and the rock roll back

Monday morning we had oatmeal for breakfast
After school Ward West kicked the piss out of me
Tuesday it snowed

Euglena

Microscopic monster
germ father, founder of the middle way
who first saw fit to join no clan
but claim the best of both
you are more than clever.

Swimming, you go to what meal is.
Green, you make what isn't.

Fencerider,

you've held your own for twenty
million years

who might have been a tulip
or a tiger

you shrewd little bastard.

The Widow

The Hammond Organ lubricates the air.
The kind mortician conducts her to her place
of honor. A man with a painted puppet's face
they say is her husband's face is obviously there

in front of her. She would have the casket
closed, but his sister would not. The minister cries
how gloriously the man is dead who lies
before him daily with a face like plastic,

prays that God who took him out of order
will keep his soul from torment, will adorn him
with a crown of stars, will hold with those that mourn him.
It is not hard, she thinks, but it will be harder.

The wail of the Hammond weakens, her mind goes black,
turning quickly out of the moment meanders
on curious ways. She looks at his nose. She wonders
if they went and slit the good blue suit in the back

and if his shoes are tied, if he has on
the socks they didn't ask for but she sent,
if they still use pennies, decides of course they don't,
hopes they will have their fill and be done with him soon.

It would not be fair to say she is not grieving.
She did not want to come, but she is aware
how there will be silence, there will be pleasures to bear
in silence, and dark creatures unbehaving.

She did not want to come. She will not be taken
to tears. But she is aware some moment will crush
the brain suddenly, that she will go home and wish
burglars had come there and the blind windows were broken.

Sale

Partnership dissolved.
Everything must be sold.
Individually or the set
as follows:

Brain, one standard, cold.
Geared to glossing.
Given to hard replies.
Convolutions convey the illusion
of exceptional depth.
Damaged.

think. you are not thinking.

One pair of eyes. Green. Like new.
Especially good for girls and women walking,
wicker baskets,
paintings by Van Gogh,
red clocks and frogs, chicken snakes and snow.

look. you are not looking.

One pair of ears, big. Best offer takes.
Tuned to Bach, Hank Williams, bees,
the Book of Job.
Shut-off for deans, lieutenants and
salesmen talking.

listen. you are not listening.

Mouth, one wide.
Some teeth missing.
Two and a half languages. Adaptable to pipes
and occasional kissing.
Has been broken but in good repair.
Lies.

tell me. why won't you tell me?

Hands, right and left.
Feet. Neck. Some hair.
Stomach, heart, spleen and
accessory parts.

Starts tomorrow
what you've been waiting for
and when it's gone it's gone.

Plain

Out of Mobile I saw a '60 Ford
fingers wrapped like pieces of rope
around the steering wheel
foxtail flapping the head of the hood
of the first thing ever
he has called his own.

Between two Bardahls
above the STP
the flag flies backwards
Go To Church This Sunday
Support Your Local Police
Post 83
They say the same thing
They say
I am not alone.

Let Me Tell You

how to do it from the beginning.
First notice everything:
The stain on the wallpaper
of the vacant house,
the mothball smell of a
Greyhound toilet.
Miss nothing. Memorize it.
You cannot twist the fact you do not know.

Remember
The blond girl you saw in the bar.
Put a scar on her breast.
Say she left home to get away from her father.
Invent whatever will support your line.
Leave out the rest.

Use metaphors: The mayor is a pig
is a metaphor
which is not to suggest
it is not a fact.
Which is irrelevant.
Nothing is less important
than a fact.

Be suspicious of any word you learned
and were proud of learning.
It will go bad.
It will fall off the page.

When your father lies
in the last light
and your mother cries for him,
listen to the sound of her crying.
When your father dies
take notes
somewhere inside.

If there is a heaven
he will forgive you
if the line you found was a good line.

It does not have to be worth the dying.

Today Is Wednesday

which is the day I have decided to understand.
I have tried since morning.
Now for the second time
my shadow is longer than I am
and still I can't understand.

I have asked everyone to help me.
I asked the busdriver to help me.
He said my name is John Foster Kelley
which is a name you will need.

I asked the waitress with mustard
on her mouth.
She said I have a surgical
scar on my belly.

I asked a policeman. I said
today is Wednesday.
He said go ask your mother.
I asked my mother.

I never saw you before in my life

son.

Tomorrow is Thursday.
Thursday I will understand.
If I can find the right bus
the right cafe
I will say
somebody help me.

Friday I will find myself
the one who can help me.

I will recognize it at once,
breasts of a big woman
face of a dog
the hinder parts held high
as a camel rises
in the unheated intergalactic spaces
under the gray blanket of my
most dry dreams

I will say *what about the whales*

and it will be done
Friday I will do it myself.

And I will tell everyone my understanding.
At first of course they will not hear
and when they do they will not allow me near
inhabited places.
I will grow old sending in scribbled notes
tied to the teats of cows and the tails of goats.

Voice of America

Do not imagine his father lying
between his mother and falling to sleep
beside her while she wonders how
she knows, knowing she will keep

the secret for a weaker proof.
Do not imagine the million seed
moving by some myotic hunger
from dark to dark, from need to need.

Do not imagine one by luck
or fate finds the target to win
and like a bullet hitting a head
in slow motion crashes in.

Do not imagine the man starts
and terminates in the same act,
will be before the bullet stops
the zero absolute unfact

his mother remembered in reverse.
Do not imagine his father sent
the million missiles against the egg
with more joy and less intent.

Do not imagine the cells splitting.
Do not imagine the hollow ball
he was awhile, a senseless worm,
no heart, head, nothing at all,

as when his father a following day
the following month would ask, "What is it?"
"It's nothing. It's honestly nothing at all."
Do not imagine the exquisite

danger when the cell divides
when a chromosome splits apart
half shifting here, half there,
to shape the kidney and the heart.

Do not imagine the enormous eyes.
Do not imagine the chin sits
soft against the uncovered heart.
Do not imagine the gill slits,

the hands unfinished, the tail shrinking.
Do not imagine the time at hand
or what it means. Raise the gun.
Hold it gently as you were trained

to hold it. Let the bullet swim
slowly into his opening head
fast as sperm   the way the films
in school can show a flower spread.

How the Elephant Got His Hump

for John Christman

Consider a fact: an olive
(unlike cherries and boysen
berries and beans) begins
as a most potent poison.

An olive grower of course
and biochemist know what'll
make it the bitter and dun
hors d'oeuvre we buy in a bottle.

The olive is soaked in lye
for twenty days and turned
on every one of the twenty
to keep it from being burned

then soaked in the juice of pickles
and turned every day
which renders the amine soluble
enough to be leached away

the amine being the problem
which amine being bound
to a protein makes an olive
which falls upon the ground

so deadly quick a poison
which is why the lye
has first to break the bond
which of course is why

no man of the Middle East
or beast has ever been seen
or seen again if he was
eating an olive green.

The question before the house:
Since the receipt is now
4,000 years old at least
who found it out, and how?

Well, I have a fancy.
Imagine the High Priest
Lord Executioner
of all the Middle East

preparing to put to death
a breaker of taboos
who diddled the temple virgins
and never paid his dues

in the shabby lodge he lived in
and pissed in the sacred pool
slept at sacrifices
and toyed with his tool

until he roused the anger
of elders and what was worse
perverse admiration
until a public curse

was said upon his head.
The High Priest swore to make
a more than common end
and set about to take

the fruit which was by custom
exquisite execution,
to cook it first in a caustic,
second an acid, solution.

When he contemplated
the agony in his hand
he could only smile
that he could understand

how he had come to be
the number one High Priest
Lord Executioner
of all the Middle East.

To make more perfect perfection
and imperfect people the humbler
he poured the *coup de grace*
two poisons in a tumbler

juice of the fruit and grain
said to drive men mad
and mixed them 5 to 1
by chance and knew he had

when he dropped in the olive
such agony in the cup
that he could scarcely speak
to summon the buglers up

to the top of the highest hill
where desert turns to sky
to summon the people in
to watch the heretic die.

The heretic being of gentle
birth albeit a fool
was set to lose his life
but would not lose his cool.

He took the drink as told to
and killed it in a swallow
and asked his host politely
if there was more to follow.

He nibbled the olive even
to take fate's roughest ration
and spat the pit at the people
and posed in a manly fashion

and was not less surprised
to find he would not die
than those prostrate about him
who called him Highest of High.

As King he showed his people
his powers were still alive
by drinking a draft of poison
each afternoon at five

for all the years of his reign
which were forty and four
and said that it was good
and often called for more

prepared of course by him
who once was Lord High Priest
who now was Royal Mixer
to the King of the Middle East.

The House in the Vacant Lot

Cutting across a vacant lot
I felt concrete under my feet
and found myself at the front door
of a house that was not there anymore.

I traced the walls by where the grass
was thin and came again to the spot
where the entrance hall had been.
I let myself as it seemed to me in

and wandered through the disappeared
and long-forgotten rooms. Some glass
and a broken brick were all that was left
of the rooms where people had kissed and slept

once alone and together once.
I thought of this and then a weird
or common thought took hold of my head:
Why do I think of the past as dead?

Am I a person present and real
walking through a house that by chance
was and is not or am I he
who am not but who will be

who steps through real and present brick?
Or am I here and the house here still?
Is some woman's heartbeat quicker
when she sees the candle flicker

in a closed room? Are we together?
Does such commingling twist and crack
windows I walk through? Does a cold fear
come? Do they wonder if I walk here?

When a glass tumbles does the mother
cross herself? Does the priest
come to say that I am Christ
or to exorcise the poltergeist?

In Your Own Words Without Lying
Tell Something Of Your Background
With Particular Attention
To Anything Relating To The Position
For Which You Are Applying.
Press Down.

Pressing down I remember
the night my father
and mother will have forgotten:
she filled the lamps in the kitchen
he slung the washing water on the ground
chickens scattered squawking;
the sound of the pump primed
the cold zinc of the dipper
water down the chin
a mumbled word
and the long yawn at last
that leaves the body hollow as a gourd
when the vegetable skin
goes brown and hard
under the thick green vines
in the dry yard
And they went to bed
the night I came together
and began.

I may have been describing the night
my grandfather
emptied himself of my father
and my never uncles.

There was no way to tell the difference
in those nights.

I think that was the first important thing.

I was covered when I was five
like Job with boils
they shaved my head
peeled the cloth away from the bed
in the morning.
The neighbors came to call
said What have you done
that God has put this affliction on your son.

When I was eleven I went to sleep
with a gothic radio underneath the quilt
the glowing grin of the dial
bright as the guilt I manufactured there.

Saturday night the Grand Old Hayride
There's A Great Speckled Bird
Flying Somewhere
But I Didn't Hear Nobody Pray.

Sunday nights I listened to the prophets,
how faith washes sins and Catholics away:

This is Brother Bob's Good Old Gospel Hour
Our time is almost
send your dimes and dollars
The Bible Man
B-I-B-L-E
We depend
to help us carry on
to the first two thousand
a plastic tablecloth
that glows
in the dark
with the face of Jesus

Imagine what your friends and neighbors will say

while the choir sings one more time
in the background softly

and tenderly Jesus is calling
O Sinner Come Home.

Monday Miss Gardner began the fifth grade
took up the marbles
let Big Butt Butler erase the board
never me
sent sealed messages to other rooms
by Salina Mae who was already starting
to have tits Walter said were got
from doing it.

O.D. showed what he had behind the gin
always after Salina Mae was gone
and Mary Sue let us look if we begged her.

Walter drowned.
O.D. is a doctor. Mary Sue married
a preacher and has children.
Salina Mae I will tell you about.

One Saturday Afternoon we made believe

That is all I can tell

On my grandfather's farm
there was a river we swam in
there was an old bell to call us back

Love Poem

Six o'clock and
the sun rises across the river.
The traffic cop wakes up and
crawls over his wife.
The naked professor will sleep another hour.
The dentist wakes up and reaches for a smoke.
The doctor reaches for the phone
and prescribes
his voice full of rust.
The shoeclerk wakes to his clock
touches himself
and lies listening to his woman in the shower.

It is midnight now in Samoa.

Nine o'clock and
the school bell rings.
Miss Gardner taps her ruler on the desk.
She calls the roll.
Oscar Carpenter is absent.
He does not like the sound of the ruler.

It is midnight now in Osaka.

Eleven o'clock:
The salesman makes his way past dogs and wheels
his knuckles already sore
hoping for bells.

On Maple Street the policeman's wife
shuts her kimono slowly and shuts the door.
On Willow Street the professor's wife
tells him about her cousin in Mineral Wells
who was also a salesman but never amounted to much.

On Juniper Street the dentist's wife
is drunk and lets him have her on the floor
says she will get a divorce
says she will see him again of course if she can.

It is midnight now in Djakarta.

Five o'clock and
the men are coming home.
The traffic cop comes home
his ears in his pockets.
The doctor comes home
the sun slipping down his forehead.
The shoeclerk comes
The uncertain knees
still fitting the sockets of his eyes.

It is midnight now in Berlin.

Six o'clock:
The streetlights come on.

It is midnight now in Bordeaux.

Ten o'clock:
In Mercy Hospital a man is dying.
His brain
squeezes all his thoughts to one thought
squeezes that to nothing
and lets go.

It is midnight now in La Paz.

Eleven o'clock:
The children are gone to bed and we are here
sitting across the room from one another
accustomed to this house
that is not ours to keep
to this world that is not ours
and to each other.

Sands run through the children in their sleep.

La Ultima Carta: A Young Wife Writes to Her Husband in the Mountains

I make a Y
brittle as dry wood.
The sputtering pen splits open
unwrites words I could not have mailed.

Saturday I sat by the lake,
pretended to read letters
that have not come.
They are too brief and tell me you are well.
I am not sure I believe them.

Under my hand, Husband,
brooms break
corn grinds to sand.

You have no faith in spirits
would claim the water
dripping from a tap at night
means nothing
that a wind coming down to the coast
out of those hills is neither alive nor dead
but I listen for signs

and forgive me this:
when the wind
brushes against the curtain
touches my sheet
I tense to feel the fingers of a ghost.

I look through my eyes in the morning mirror
afraid I will conjure you
trying to conjure you there
but all I see are the days spinning back
with the strange quiet violence of dreams.

Sra. Cortinez whose son was a good soldier
is also alone and knows she is going
to be alone. I envy her knowing
for certain. Forgive me.

I sit up late
after unweaving myself
and write you letters
and every time the thought comes
that you may go and I not
know about it

that I may write a month
after your death
to tell you things
as one talks meaningfully with gestures
to a friend who half a block back
has stopped at some store,
that I will hold your picture
focus on your mouth
to remember you more
while in some obscene place
a snake is crawling through your face.

I tell you my unfaithfulness
my unforgivable sin
that I am no longer sure my letters
keep you alive

but I will keep on writing
until we win
what we are fighting for
whoever we are.

Thinking Friday Night
with a Gothic Storm Going About
Final Causes and Logos and
Mitzi Mayfair

Was the Word and the Word was just
a swelling in the ether. Dust

that would seem wind, sun, earth and sea
had not come to seem to be

and ether was only force compacted.
So are we. Though we have acted

like Stuff, we know that we are not.
We are spume and a sunspot.

This man that seems to know its name
is a water spout, a flame,

a whirlpool, a funnel storm
where nothing stays except the form

the funnel is. We are nothing
but energy in love, come huffing

and puffing our way through what we take
as time and space, as wine and steak.

This is philosophy I think
and science and a waste of ink.

And still I know the shape I touch
that seems something is nothing much,

is only a moving, and we are dreams
we have about us. The earth that seems

rocks and water is only force
moving through a shape. The source,

they will say, of rhyme and the seasons
but we have our own good reasons

for holding to the old confusions
of form and thing. What but illusions

matter at all when all things
are what they do? A wasp's wings,

for instance, and you, as I am a node
energy moves through, coming as food

drink, salt, sunlight, air,
and leaving as heat, spit, hair,

tears, toenails, words and sperm.
Lord bless the lowly worm

who is also form in flux
and does not know or care and fucks

such as he does without the stinking
thoughts we always come to thinking.

Darling, let us learn to move
like that again—apparent you

force and form, *vis-à-vis*
form and force, apparent me—

riding the storm all words are about
till the storm stops, played out.

Vision and Prayer

Christ that as the maggot
Takes unto himself our putrefaction
Cleanse us now and in the hour of our death

Christ that as the maggot
Comes not for the clean
Cleanse us now and in the hour of our death

Christ that as the maggot
Comes from the grave and grows wings
Cleanse us now and in the hour of our death

Christ that as the maggot
Is with us always
Cleanse us now and in the hour of our death

Maggot of God that eats away
The corruption of the world
Cleanse Bless us now and in the hour of our death

Sitting Alone at Sunrise: Problems in the Space-Time Continuum

If in the future
a time traveler
comes back to this moment
he's here now.

Say that from 10,000 feet you see a car
run off a country road and turn over.
It's already a county away.
Take the coffee.

There will come a year
when one by one your friends
thumbing past your last address
will think to mark through it.

If I could be
in two places at once
I would be with you twice
all the time.

On the Symbolic Consideration of Hands and the Significance of Death

Watch people stop by bodies in funeral homes.
You know their eyes will fix on the hands and they do.
Because a hand that has no desire to make
a fist again or cut bread or lay stones
is among those things most difficult to believe.
It is believed for a fact by a very few
old nuns in France who carve beads out of knuckle bones.

I Go Out of the House for the First Time

I go out of the house for the first time
since the day everybody found out
and the first person I meet says hello turd
so I pull off my ears I have always had
distinctive ears and drop them in a trash
dispenser in front of The Farmers Bank and a man
coming out of the bank says hello turd
so I twist off my nose as people have always
noticed my nose in particular and drop it in
the book deposit in front of the city library
and a woman coming out of the library says
hello turd and I begin to see
how difficult disguises are and pluck
my left eye out as people have always noticed
my eyes are most particularly well matched
and swallow it down as there is no place to put it
and a small boy up a lamp pole says
hello turd so I take off my clothes
as people have always commented on my clothes
and I walk down the street and a little girl
playing jacks on the sidewalk sees me and says
hello turd so I pull off my penis
and everybody runs up saying in loud voices
look at the dumb turd he pulled off his penis

And Then

Your toothbrush won't remember your mouth
Your shoes won't remember your feet

Your wife one good morning
will remember your weight
will feel unfaithful
throwing the toothbrush away
dropping the shoes in the Salvation Army box
will set your picture in the living room

Someone wearing a coat you would not have worn
will ask was that your husband
she will say yes

A Toast to Floyd Collins

To Mitzi Mayfair
To Jesus Christ Man of A Thousand Faces
To Lev Davidovich Trotsky
To Nicanor Parra

To whoever dies tonight in New Orleans
To Operator 7 in Kansas City

To the sound of a car crossing a wooden bridge
To the Unified Field Theory
To the Key of F

And while I'm at it
A toast to Jim Beam
To all the ice cubes thereunto appertaining
To Jordan knitting
A silver cat asleep in her lap
And the sun going down

Which is the explanation for everything

Everything Is Fine Here How Are You

She blinks above her sunglasses at the man
putting the letters up on the movie marquee.
Along the wire he slides an S, an N.
His sleeves are cut away. The marguerita
she presses against her mouth. She feels her mouth
suck in against the salt. She watches the man
test his way descending the stepladder
and jerk it spraddled across the sidewalk.
The sound has her in front of a shingled house,
her mother pushing the screendoor open, calling
always. She watches him climb the ladder again.
If she passes that way and speaks to him
he will go off and leave her in a grove of oaks,
the twisted bra knotted about her wrists,
the panties stuffed in her mouth, the eyes
her own eyes paying no attention.

Reading the Newspaper on Microfilm

I let it go for the fact of it fast as it will
pages and days sliding by in a gray blur
black spaces falling before the headlines
marking the nights and mornings until I can tell
Sundays by their length and the running colors
department store ads from news from real estate
by normal sequence and shifting densities.
I almost wonder if I watched it long enough,
could I tell the car wrecks from the weddings,
weddings from rapes and fires and book reviews.
The names in accidents and baseball scores
for months pass by in minutes. I see
that I have stayed from April into autumn
and think of a mind that saw it all go by
as fast as that in the first place and wonder at it.

On Hearing About the Death
of Mitzi Mayfair

Hurrah for the next
man that dies
said Errol Flynn
and someone
snuk open the earth
and let him in.

Jesus died legend has it on dogwood
whose blossom for that reason
cursed itself into a cross.
The small red spot
at the tip of each plain petal
spread just at the Easter season
we say is the blood but it isn't.
You know it's not.

I close my eyes and see a calendar
with a date circled in red.

The trouble is that
my madness
was not the other half
of your madness.

There has never been a poem
to explain anything.
For that reason
many people who would otherwise
write poems do not.
Praise such people.

On the Way Home from Nowhere,
New Year's Eve

For papers I think I need, we bump off
the street and stop. I leave the engine on,
mean to make my way to the buzzing light
above the back door, but the door is dark.
Old Main's a hulking, dull, uncertain form,
no windows and no size. Then I remember

one small truth I didn't mean to remember,
that all the lights at ten would be turned off
for somebody's purpose. I enter the hollow form,
try one time to flick the light switch on
and shrug my way into the seamless dark.
What outside seemed scattered, useless light

would be a brilliance here. Reflections. Moonlight.
Sensing my way between the walls I remember
old mythologies of daytime and the dark
spun by gods and monster movies, cast off
with ignorance. My fingers stumble on
another switch. Nothing. I feel my form

falling away into another form.
I hear the hound, look for the quick light
glancing out of his eyes and imagine my own
open, aimless, milky. I remember
what children think of when the lights are off.
Something brushing the hand. To fit the dark

I tell myself I am blind. In such a dark
I could be moving down the spaceless form
of time, a painted tunnel. I twist off
my shoes and walk in deafness. Leap. Grow light
for one slow moment, then loose parts remember
gravity. I twist the sounds back on.

I'm over a million years old and going on
thirteen. I've always been afraid of the dark.
There truly are warlocks, witches, and I remember
banshees, saints and the always shifting form
of Satan himself. I feel a fly light
and crawl across my forehead. I brush it off.

Going on, I grab some papers off
some desk in the dark and turn back toward the light
I barely remember, running, hungry for form.

Picker

Uvalde Texas to Nashville Tennessee
is near as a tavern jukebox, is twice as far
as Jesus to Judas, as a rusty Plymouth car
to a bus with a bedroom. We look outside to see

hundreds come honking to listen to whistle to praise
the picker among us, come to tell us again
about the differences, as mostly between
how we imagine marriage those quick days

till we do marry, and how we learn to live
together after with the debts and beer
and strangers' crotches open everywhere.
I watch to learn the life you learn to give

to tell the love and sickness in our skin
and neon lights and darkness. Lord we crave
those words for hardness of our bones, to save
the soul from puffiness. You put us in

flat touch with what we are, and make that touch
bearable first, then almost pleasant and then
plain necessary, how we try to mend
our nervous ways for nothing and drink too much

and want bad love. I listen to you sing
while lean red faces eat you up alive
to know by what bright secrets we survive
the flesh's soft transgressions. No rhyming thing

will give the sense men want of who they are.
Or undo the differences we didn't mean
to deal with once—as for instance between
the bus with the bedroom and the rusty car.

Which is a green distance and does grow
while the car in the side mirror shrinks away
and you want to touch the driver's shoulder and say
Man, we're going too fast. You don't though.

Memphis, 2 P.M.

I saw a woman getting out of a car.
She said to the man in the car
leave me alone.
She closed the door with both hands.
She said to the man please
just leave me alone.

It was a new Plymouth,
blue with a white top.

Husband

She's late. He mixes another drink.
He turns on the television and watches
a woman kissing the wrong man.
He looks at his watch. He feels close
to the cat. Well Cat, he says.
He feels foolish.
He mixes another drink and stands
turning the stem of the glass
back and forth in his fingers.
This also makes him feel foolish.
He looks at his watch. Well Cat, he says.
Lights turn into the driveway.
He slumps into his chair. He
kicks off his shoes and spreads
the open newspaper peacefully
over his face.
He hears the tiny grating of the key.
His heart knocks to get out.

After You Die You Don't Give
a Piddling Damn

I do, Lord, I do. Therefore I am.

How to Stop Smoking

If you are a man
think of a woman wiggling out of her underwear
saying come on you don't have to love me.

If you are a woman
think of the man thinking that.

Practice.

How Does a Madsong Know
That's What It Is?

If vampires do suck blood, if space is time,
if there is a hell for sins and heaven for virtues,
if the dead do remember, if once witches
did visit with the devil and did come
to Massachusetts when the devil came,
if matter turns to light as it approaches
the speed of light it therefore never reaches,
if Tanna leaves lead home, or the pentagram,
all these are carnival tricks. What is a ghost,
a resurrection, a warp in time, a hell,
beside the fact that we do seem to exist?
What idiot believes in anything?
What idiot is there who doesn't believe it all
With heigh! The sweet birds! Oh, how they sing!

Why God Permits Evil:
For Answer to This Question
of Interest to Many
Write Bible Answers Dept. E–7

—ad on a matchbook cover

Of interest to John Calvin and Thomas Aquinas
for instance and Job for instance who never got

one straight answer but only his cattle back.
With interest, which is something, but certainly not

any kind of answer unless you ask
God if God can demonstrate God's power

and God's glory, which is not a question.
You should all be living at this hour.

You had Servetus to burn, the elect to count,
bad eyes and the Institutes to write;

you had the exercises and had Latin,
the hard bunk and the solitary night;

you had the neighbors to listen to and your woman
yelling at you to curse God and die.

Some of this to be on the right side;
some of it to ask in passing, Why?

Why badness makes its way in a world He made?
How come he looked for twelve and got eleven?

You had the faith and looked for love, stood pain,
learned patience and little else. We have E–7.

Churches may be shut down everywhere,
half-written philosophy books be tossed away.

Some place on the south side of Chicago
a lady with wrinkled hose and a small gray

bun of hair sits straight with her knees together
behind a teacher's desk on the third floor

of an old shirt factory, bankrupt and abandoned
except for this just cause, and on the door:

Dept. E–7. She opens the letters
asking why God permits it and sends a brown

plain envelope to each return address.
But she is not alone. All up and down

the thin and creaking corridors are doors
and desks behind them: E–6, E–5, 4, 3.

A desk for every question, for how we rise
blown up and burned, for how the will is free,

for when is Armageddon, for whether dogs
have souls or not and on and on. On

beyond the alphabet and possible numbers
where cross-legged, naked and alone,

there sits a pale, tall and long-haired woman
upon a cushion of fleece and eiderdown

holding in one hand a hand-written answer,
holding in the other hand a brown

plain envelope. On either side, cobwebbed
and empty baskets sitting on the floor

say *in* and *out*. There is no sound in the room.
There is no knob on the door. Or there is no door.

The Friend

I hadn't seen him in twelve years.
He could put his hands between the wall
and a light and make a rollercoaster
a kidney machine a split T
running a double reverse.
I heard he was in town so of course I invited him.
I took down a picture to have a blank space
on the wall.
Everyone gathered in a semicircle.
I turned off all the lights except one lamp.
Go ahead I said.
He made a dog.
Then he made a rabbit. It only had one ear.
The elephant didn't have a trunk
and looked like a cow.
Jesus Christ I said What happened.
I could hear someone across the room
mixing a drink in the dark.

Getting Experience

The first real job I had was delivering drugs
for Jarman's Pharmacy in Bascum, Arkansas.

If everyone was busy or in the back I sold things.
A cloudy woman with pentecostal hair

softly asked for sanitary napkins.
She brought the Kleenex back unwrapped in twenty minutes.

Shame said Mr. Jarman, we shouldn't make a joke
of that and made me say I'm sorry and fired me.

When I found out what the woman wanted
I had to say I did what everyone said I did.

That or let them know I hadn't heard of Kotex.
Better be thought bad than known for stupid.

The first hard fight I had was after school
with Taylor Wardlow West in Bascum, Arkansas.

Ward West chased me home from school when I was lucky.
My father said Ward West was insecure.

Go smile at him he said and let him know
you mean to be his friend. My father believed in love.

All day I smiled and twisted in my seat to see him
all hate and slump by himself in the back of the room.

After school he sat on my chest and hit me
and then his little brother sat on my chest and hit me.

And then his little sister sat on my chest and hit me.
She made me so ashamed I tried to kick her

and kicked Ward West in the face. When he could see
I was rounding the corner for home. Jesus, Jesus, Jesus.

Next day everybody told me over and over
how I had balls to make those stupid faces,

him the son of a bitch of the whole school
and how I surely did kick the piss out of him.

Ward had to go to the dentist. Also his father beat him.
He didn't come to school for two days.

Then he left me alone. He said I was crazy.
Everybody thought I was a little crazy.

Although with balls. I just let them say I was.
Better be thought mad than known for stupid.

Sneeze, belch or fart. Choose if you have a choice.
Nobody's going to think you're good and sane and smart.

Being Here

The ring of a doorbell
at three in the morning
even before you know who's standing out there
changes not only the face that flies into your head
but shoes also and the backs of chairs and the repetitions
of wallpaper.
You may say a quick prayer
but anyway you will take it as you have to.

Notes from the Agent on Earth:
How to be Human

In St. Peter's Basilica in the City of Rome
there sits a holy father fashioned in marble
encircled by faces well proportioned and doubtless.
His name is Gregory; he spoke for God.
He sits upon a slab; under that slab
the devil, winged and dog-faced, cat-pawed and crooked,
turns in his agony and bares his teeth,
bares his broken claws, turns his nostrils
almost inside out. The statue is his.
One purchases with popes and attendant angels
the privilege of discovering such a devil.
No one could dare to show him by himself.
This loser, this bad and living dream, this Lucifer
alone is more than all the hovering others.
Because he carries folded into his face
what no face erased in heaven carries,
the fear and loneliness to make us human.
All there is to understand is there.
None here has anything to share with angels.
What makes a human human (more than speech,
a pair of opposable thumbs or the set of the head)
is a cold hand that reaches from under the bed
and closes on your ankle; is lying awake
flat on your back in bed and becoming aware
your hands are coffin-crossed upon your chest,
not having the little courage to leave them there.
And the girl in the hotel lobby, lost in her fat,
forgetting the room of the man who likes her like that.
The woman with buttons on her back undone
to show she doesn't live with anyone.
Think of men and women in nursing homes.
These were senators, some of them, and bankers,
presidents of colleges, detectives,
people who passed laws, wrote books,
gave loans, found clues, presided over professors,
crying all night in thin metal beds for their mothers,
calling in high voices daddy daddy,
and mother and daddy dead for thirty years.

What we have in common and what we know
from Loneliness and Fear, called Adam and Eve,
and all we have to turn our hands to
are Love, Ambition, Faith, the Sense of Death.

Love is Fear and Loneliness fed and sleeping;
Faith is Fear and Loneliness explained,
denied and dealt in; Ambition which is envy
is Fear and Loneliness coming up to get you;
Death is Fear and Loneliness fading out.
This is the stuff of life and the gospel of art.
So art and life are much alike in this.
But art, because we see both ends, can please us.
We never know if life is a cave or a tunnel.
We only know we spend the days going deeper,
half in fucking or hunting flesh to fuck
and half philosophizing the fuck away
with talk about the nature of good and evil,
which is a waste of energy and time.
The only question with any answer that matters
is whether we have a little free will or none.

But this is only content; this is stuffing.
Flesh is distastefully still and marble is rock
without the patterns a body pushes through.
So life and art are much alike in this.
Life is change that finds a changing pattern,
says the pither of frogs and cat-slitter;
art is change we put a pattern to.
And so is sport and war and merchandising.
There is a difference but it doesn't matter.

The old nun who believes in nothing
crosses herself sitting down to supper
and men and women living in New Orleans
dress in the brown and orange clothes of autumn
one certain heavy, indistinguishable day.
They call this The First Day Of Autumn.
Some women in Messina whose times of mourning
come close together and touch and overlap
wear black into black the last ten years of their lives.

This is about Love and how to tell it.
Charles Hammond Walker of South Carolina,
son of Charles and Sue born Sue Ella Hammond,
daughter of Colonel John and Martha Hammond
of Tennessee, got off a plane in Chicago
and got a taxi and got a hotel room
and got a badge and got a daily paper
and went to a movie house that shows movies
of naked people doing reciprocal things,
remembered when he got inside the movie
to put the plastic badge that had the name
Charles Hammond Walker in his pocket,
sat down and spread the paper across his lap,
took his penis and pulled it out of his pants
into the cool air. Charles Hammond Walker
has a wife who sometimes in South Carolina
goes dreaming up a chance, a quick chance.

There are many stories of contented lovers.
Some people believe them; be careful of these.
The best counsel is likely of no account.

One says: I love you and you alone. One says:
I have something to tell you. Please sit down.

This is about Faith and how to tell it.
Think if you saw a ghost you knew was a ghost.
All the questions answered by that knowledge
are questions of Faith, though this defeats the question.
Faith justified by fact is no faith.

Newspapers, no matter how final the news is,
invite subscriptions, which—though business—
is an act of faith in delay, in possibly not.

One says: The Lord is with us. One says:
There is a fountain filled with blood. Amen.

This is about the Will to Power, Envy,
Covetousness, Ambition, maker of popes,
wars, weddings, poems, and county fairs.

A private holding a microphone like a scepter
can bring commanding generals to silence.

Or start with the swollen moment, the blimp saying yes,
the drum major pumping like a piston,
the majorettes spinning their silver spokes,
pulling the band behind them, dividing the crowd;
cables connecting vans to high windows
cameras scanning the street. Look at the man
putting money into the parking meter.
Watch how the meter runs down, watch how the band
puts down its instruments and disappears,
how the vans pull away, look how the broken cables
go leaping behind them, look how the people leave,
the last ones on the last bus standing silent.
Look at the man with his hand on the parking meter.
Look at his shoulder, slick with pigeon drippings.
Watch how the pigeons fly away and come back.

Say some people are tourists. They go to Pompeii.
They are unhappy there. They frequently stumble.
Back in the bus they sit astonished and grieve.
It's hard to believe, Well it's hard to believe.
They are not grieving for Pompeii.

One says: He slipped away in the night. One says:
Everybody move up to the next desk.

This is about Death and how to tell it.

When a man looks down at the back of his hand
and sees the hand of his father he knows he is dying.

One says: Listen. When I was very young
my father took me out to see the mountains.
We renamed all the animals we saw
with words no one had ever put together
and then we forgot them. My father is long dead.

Much that is said of the dead is bullshit.

One says: Listen. It gets sweet close to the end.
It is very important not to be dead.

The eyes of people in the last hours are bright.

The Lord giveth, the Lord taketh away.
One says: Please Lord. And so much for that.

This is also something about Ambition.
Also Love. And Faith also. And Death.

A man who had too much to calculate
had a vision of hell, was afraid of the dark,
knew that he had walked in evil ways,
corrected his wife to death and darkened his children;
had done things besides unspeakably bad
and could not honestly ask for God's forgiveness
as he was only afraid and could never say
I'm sorry, Lord. He wanted such redemption
as wipes a life not clean but wipes it away.
And thought that he could have it. He spent his means
for fifteen years of the best brains to be had
in mathematics, space-time and madness
and had him when he was eighty by god
a simple time-machine, which ought not now
bend any imagination out of shape;
went back seventy years to the same town
and found himself at ten delivering papers;
stole the one car there was and ran himself down;
left himself across a wooden sidewalk,
who barely lied to his mother or masturbated,
and went directly to heaven if any can.
He could not be the man who killed the boy
because he never lived to be the man,
having died at ten delivering papers,
survived by his parents, grieved by the fifth grade,
the first death by car in the whole county,
killed by a runaway Ford with no driver
or if a driver, none to be found.

There is much that matters. What matters most is survival.
What matters most in survival is learning the names
of things and the names of visions. If the horizon
for an example were real someone could go there
and call back to the rest of us and say
Here we are standing on the horizon.
But he would see that his friends were standing on it.

No sense of space or time is dependable here.
The difference in time is that we glance back
at those who stayed in time and didn't come with us,
and see ourselves still back there talking to them.
These are illusions, or seem to be illusions.
Leave them alone. What matters most is survival.

One says: Fuck you, Jack. One says: Up yours.
Climb on that and rotate, motherfucker.
Why can't I go? Everybody's going.
I didn't hardly touch you for godsake.

Be careful of too much imagination.
This attracts attention. Attention is trouble.
You have to develop competence, of course.
You have to think of doors opening toward you.
Take any pleasure in it and sooner or later
someone will notice your eyes have an absent look.
Someone with a glass in her hand will stop talking
and wait for you to answer. Practice caution.
Tell stories at parties the way you hear them. .

Be careful of how the night moves into morning.
When things have gone right the day opens and closes,
one calendar square checked off and done with.
When something is wrong, when you've drunk too much
or had a fight over love or lost money,
the night runs into the morning in sick streaks
like the fluids of a dog run over in the last block.

Be careful of uniforms of any color,
of glass doors with initials painted on them,
of people always willing to go last.
Be careful of workers who have their own desks.
Be very careful of people whose young are hungry
and have large faces, of days set aside
for the celebration of national independence,
of those who are neither lonely nor afraid.

Be careful everywhere. This is a world—
what?—divided. Not as they say divided.
Think of this: running around the planet,
along the equator exactly, an iron fence;
half the population of the planet
stands on either side and shakes the bars
screaming to be let out, to be let in.

Main Street

We came here to live in a small town.
Already the bypass half-encircles us,
the three-story houses on Maple Street are gone
except for one which is a funeral home
with sad blue blinking letters over the porch.

The streets are guarded by two-headed parking meters
which doesn't matter since half the stores closed down
after Sears and Penney's moved to the mall.

Now something neither town nor city takes over.
The hospital adds a wing. The census swells.
The city limits signs of six towns
move toward each other like suspicious children.

Our children whom we meant to raise as hicks
come strangely into the house and bring new words.
They are well bred and come from good stock.
They join us always for breakfast. We see in their eyes
and in their smiles they are patient and willing to wait.

Waiting for the Paper to be Delivered

Late January.
Snow is on everything.
No matter how far I listen there is only silence.

Two yellow machines have worked for a week
cutting away the hill in front of the house
I have come to live in for the rest of my life.

On the highest part of the hill
one oak is standing.

Nothing else is vertical on the horizon.
It locks the white sky to the white earth.

Fly Me to the Moon

He learns what love can do and what it can't do.
He sees it in her face more than he wants to.

He recognizes the interrogative touch
he can't decipher and doesn't like too much.

Sometimes they do lie down together
and feel at home in the grace of one another.

This is not what he thought it would be,
but nothing else is, either. She would agree.

The Survivor

According to the helicopter pilot,
the staticky talk on the two-way radio,
the next crest and the next
up a dry wash a mile or so
and there: the tail fin first, a wing, unusual odors.
No one seems to be alive but a woman,
standing as still as the topless trees,
her left arm hanging loose in the crusted sleeve.

"What are your thoughts on being the sole survivor?"
says the reporter, stumbling beside the stretcher.

Says the lady, "Sir—," and then the stretcher slips
and she slides free and falls a hundred feet,
tumbling down the mountain, loosening rocks.

Some say the red ribbon she had in her hair
fluttered loose when she fell and was found
almost at once
by a large bird, white, or more gray than white.

The Well-Ordered Life

Once he went inside a pool hall.
The clicking billiard balls put him in mind
of African tribes who click to say, "I love you"
"What do you want?" "We're going to kill you, of course."
They skirted the circles of light in a secret frenzy.

He took his Instamatic every week
and thirty-five dollars to life class.
He didn't use film. He couldn't have hidden the pictures.
He circled and focused and framed. The breast and knee.
The purest art he said is the briefest art.

Once he hunted for love. A long time
he stood beside a little fat lady,
dressed in red, standing on the corner,
looking something like a fire hydrant.
She boarded a bus and left him there alone.

Daily the desperate ordering of this world,
the objects on his desk, the chosen words,
the knife, fork and spoon, the folded napkin,
the one, two, three, the counting, counting,
a constant laying of sandbags on the levee.

Getting the Message

Hermes it was. Hermes with wingéd heels,
looking like an ad for FTD.
I woke to see his silhouetted frame
inside the window frame. Hermes it was.
With, I had to assume, a message for me.

He wore the same hard hat he always wore,
suggesting a nudist on a construction crew,
except the hat had wings. Except also,
he wasn't entirely nude. The ribbon flapped
and did precisely what it was meant to do.

Not meaning to seem a churl, a poor host,
or wanting to seem too easily surprised
by this event, this hour of the morning
here in a Houston hotel, and thus appear
outside of myth and thus uncivilized,

and on the other hand, not wanting to seem
so gullible as to think the man was there
if it should turn out later he never was,
I lay in a shape that may have been described
if I were standing up as devil-may-care.

The hat's wings fluttered once. He shifted the hat.
"My name," he said, "is Hermes." "I know," I said.
I figured I could give him credence enough
for a civil response, at which response he entered
and scooted my feet aside and sat on the bed.

He asked if I was me. I said I was,
but I was not the one about whom doubt
might naturally arise and did he suppose
I'd be convinced as easily as that.
"Convincing you is not what I came about."

The tone was matter-of-fact. "I have a message."
"I take it you do," I said, "if you're in fact
an entity." "I have a message for you
whether I'm an entity or not.
There's no need for rudeness." "So how do I act

.

when Hermes comes in the window? Please understand
I'm trying to keep a fix on what we call
the phenomenological world. It isn't easy."
"That's what the message is about," he said.
"I'll have to have your promise, first of all,

not to tell anybody about the visit."
"What possible difference," I said, "could it make to you?
Nobody would believe it." "No difference," he said.
"It's like the apple, or never looking back.
There has to be something you're not allowed to do."

"How do you know I'll do what I say?" I said.
"When I tell about it—were I to—
I'd know already what the message is."
"So you would," he said. "But in that case,
whatever I tell you turns out not to be true."

He plucked a quill and pulled from under his hat
a packet of papers. "If you would please sign here."
I signed the promise. He rose in a flurry of wings.
The message, in a swirling cursive, read
What ought to happen happens in one year.

Mythic people like that sort of thing.
They tell you something that looks fine at first.
I've pondered it these past eleven months.
Now it's told, untold, there's nothing to tell.
Whatever it saved us from, or what it cost,
whether I lost us heaven, or spared us hell,
a die's uncast, a Rubicon uncrossed.

Ghosts

Some evenings, there are ghosts. There are. Ghosts
come in through the door when people come in,
being unable to open doors themselves
and not knowing (not knowing they are ghosts)

they could pass through anything, like thought.
They come and stand, move aimlessly about
as if each one of them had come to meet
someone who hadn't arrived. I always thought

of haunts and spirits as having a special power
like witches to do whatever they wanted to.
They don't. Pure energy without a cage
can do nothing at all. Whatever power

pushes or pulls the things of this world
to any purpose does it by piston or pistol,
mill wheel or spring or some such pushing back.
Spirit freed fades into the world.

Inertia, which is habit, holds their lines
a little while and then like memories
they weaken and fade. The glow is energy going.
They seem like actors trying to remember lines.

The trouble is they don't know they're dead.
We don't know very much about ghosts;
we think that some of those who aren't prepared
and die surprised don't understand they're dead.

They hang around. The kindest thing to do
when you see one is simply to say
"Listen, you're dead. You're dead. Get out of here."
That's what the ghost eventually will do

when we've told it again and again to go.
"Get out of here. Get out of here. You're dead."
They can't of course go anywhere on purpose;
you have to give them intent to make them go.

And who knows where? All this has to do
with Newton's laws. The figure disappears.
Somewhere there's a place. Be kind. Be firm.
Remember the only thing you have to do

is tell them the truth. Say "You're dead. Get out."
Ignore the slow confusion on their faces.
Never pity. They can soak up pity.
Sympathy makes them denser and drags it out.

If pity comes, don't let it go to them.
Watch for a sudden change in temperature.
You still have a death to deal with.
Pity yourself, who could be one of them

to live—as it were—with all the embarrassment.
You would not want someone who sounds like
a movie director telling you you're dead.
Your tissue hands could not hide the embarrassment.

Late Show

Too tired to sleep I switch a picture on,
Turn down the sound to let my attention drain.
A forest in summer. Dogs. A man is running.
It's starting to rain.

The man comes to a house. He breaks a window.
A girl getting out of the shower admiring herself
looks to see if the cat has knocked something
from the kitchen shelf.

She sees the man. She wraps a towel about her.
In the woods loosed from their leashes the dogs
are running in circles scratching at empty trees
sniffing at logs.

The woman is breathing behind a chair in the kitchen.
The man is leaning against the kitchen door.
Her mouth moves. He hits her in the face.
She falls to the floor.

He tears the towel away. He stands above her.
He looks a long time. He lets her curl
into a corner. Both of us can see
she is only a girl.

He takes her to her bed and drops her in it.
Looks at her as if he has not seen her
before now. Takes off his clothes and puts
himself between her.

He moves his lips. She bends her legs and locks him.
They move together. I turn up the sound.
They stop moving. They look in my direction.
A single hound

is crouping close. She shoves the man aside,
rolls out of bed, runs with nothing around her
into the rain, into the leaping dogs.
Lightning and thunder.

He sits on the bed, his back a slow curve.
Turn it off, he says, in god's name.
The door opens. A man with a long gun.
He takes aim.

Trying to Remember

You know in the muddy pond the fish is there.
It bumps the bait and late in the long shadows
it nudges a brief circle over the surface.
Give it up. It will die in the dark water.

The Ones That Are Thrown Out

One has flippers. This one is like a seal.
One has gills. This one is like a fish.
One has webbed hands, is like a duck.
One has a little tail, is like a pig.
One is like a frog
with no dome at all above the eyes.

They call them bad babies.

They didn't mean to be bad
but who does.

Form and Theory of Poetry

Think of how in a hurricane the winds
build up from nothing at all and suddenly stop
then start the opposite way and die down,
the way the traffic around a stadium
builds to the game, stops, starts again
going the other direction, dies down.
Think in the eye of a hurricane, then, of Tittle,
Thorpe and Namath, Simpson, such acts of God.
At a football game, think of the Gulf coast,
Biloxi, Mississippi blown away.

Words

Strip to the waist and have a seat. The doctor
will be in soon. He smiles and the nurse smiles.
He sits on the table, bumping his knees together,
scratching around his navel, counting the tiles.

We never talk, she says, and so you talk
and everything you speak of falls apart.
This is how we come to understand
what they mean by chambers of the heart.

Some words are said to start a conversation.
Some, after which there's nothing more to say.
"Amen," for instance. "I said I was sorry."
"Tower, we're going down. This is PSA."

Style

Sometimes he would try to write a poem
and what he wanted to do was scribble circles
down one side of the page and up the other
and once he did but he knew it wasn't a poem
although there were those who would have called it one
assuming of course that it was done sincerely.

Not wanting to waste the paper or the time
and having a dean impressed by anything,
he titled and signed it and sent it off
and there it was in the Golden Rule Review,
"Poem in Sincere Circles." It was sincere.
A few months later it got anthologized.

He sits at his desk devising variations,
starting in the center of the page,
circles in circles with small symbols in them.
He publishes everywhere and gets letters
asking for explanations he never gives.
Also he never gives readings anymore.

Believing in Symbols

1

One morning I put in the pocket of my shirt
not having put two and two together
a little calculator. That afternoon
it lay on my desk and turned out 8s for hours,
shorted through by those rippling shocks
the sinus node sends out, now beat, now beat.

So what do we say for science and the heart?
So with reason the heart will have its way?

Believing in symbols has led us into war,
if sometimes into bed with interesting people.

2

8 becomes in the time of solid state
the figure all the figures are made from,
the enabling number, the all-fathering 8;
1 through 7, also nothing and 9,
are all pieces of 8 which is only itself.

This makes a certain sense if you look at the sign
that says infinity, the Möbius strip,
a lazy 8 hung on the gates of heaven.

The pterodactyl, Pompeii, the Packard;
things take their turns. 3 and 7 are only
numbers again. Nothing stays for long.
Not to say that physics will ever fail us
or plain love, either, for that matter.
Like the sides of a coin, they may take turns,
or flipping fast enough, may seem to merge.

Call it, if you call it, in the air.
When the coin comes down, the tent comes down.
You look around, and there is nothing there.
Not even the planets. Not even the names of the planets.

Love and How It Becomes Important
in Our Day to Day Lives

The man who tells you which is the whiter wash,
the woman who talks about her paper towels,
the woman whose coffee holds her home together,
the man who smells the air in his neighbor's house,

the man who sings a song about his socks,
the woman who tells how well her napkin fits,
the man who sells the four-way slicer-dicer,
the woman who crosses tape between her tits,

and scores besides trample my yard, a mob
demanding to be let in, like Sodomites
yelling to get at my guests but I have no guests.
I crawl across the floor and cut the lights.

"We know you're there," they say. "Open the door."
"Who are you?" I say. "What do you want with me?"
"What does it matter?" they say. "You'll let us in.
Everyone lets us in. You'll see. You'll see."

The chest against the door begins to give.
I settle against a wall. A window breaks.
I cradle a gun in the crook of my elbow.
I hear the porch collapse. The whole house shakes.

Then comes my wife as if to wake me up,
a case of ammunition in her arms.
She settles herself against the wall beside me.
"The towns are gone," she says. "They're taking the farms."

Pity and Fear

In westerns the man who saddles up at night
is not going to say goodbye to someone
pretending to be asleep in the still cabin.

Which is to say he loves her and didn't mean to.
All she knows about him are dusty lies.
He stopped here to give his horse some water.

Or so he said. He stopped. It doesn't matter.
The man who saddles up his horse knows something.
What about her man? Will he not know?

Oh he will know, though he will never say it.
He will know his wife is not his woman.
He will become the sheriff and be a good one.

We see a passing of years. The man returns.
A windy desert town he barely remembers.
The tall son of the sheriff is dark and quick.

He gambles some. The women like him. His name
is Larry or Jim. He has his mother's eyes.
We know what will happen. Still we sit. We wait.

Evening: A Studio in Rome

The window here is hung in the west wall.
It lays on the opposite wall a square of light.
Sliced by the lopsided slats of the broken blind,
the light hangs like a painting. Now, and now,
the shadow of a swallow shoots across it.

I turn around to see the birds themselves,
scores of birds, hundreds, a thousand swallows.
I try to keep a single bird. I lose it.
In all that spinning not one bird spins loose.

I turn away from the window and back to work.
My eyes are caught again by the square of light.
I lean back in my chair and watch the picture
moving up the wall, the single birds
living out their lives in a frame of light,
until it touches the ceiling and fades out.
I turn around again and the swallows are gone.
The sun is gone. This minute Rome is dark
as only Rome is dark, as if somebody
could go out reaching toward it, and find no Rome.

Rubaiyat for Sue Ella Tucker

Sue Ella Tucker was barely in her teens.
She often minded her mother. She didn't know beans
About what boys can do. She laughed like air.
Already the word was crawling up her jeans.

Haskell Trahan took her for a ride
Upon his motorbike. The countryside
Was wet and beautiful and so were they.
He didn't think she'd let him but he tried.

They rode along the levee where they hid
To kiss a little while and then he slid
His hand inside her panties. Lord lord.
She didn't mean to let him but she did.

And then she thought that she would go to hell
For having let befall her what befell,
More for having thought it rather nice.
And she was sure that everyone could tell.

Sunday morning sitting in the pew
She prayed to know whatever she should do
If Haskell Trahan who she figured would
Should take her out again and ask her to.

For though she meant to do as she was told
His hands were warmer than the pew was cold
And she was mindful of him who construed
A new communion sweeter than the old.

Then sure enough, no matter she would try
To turn her head away and start to cry,
He had four times before the week was out
All of her clothes and all his too awry.

By then she'd come to see how she had learned
As women will a lesson often earned:
Sweet leads to sweeter. As a matter of fact,
By then she was not overly concerned.

Then in the fullness of time it came to be
That she was full of child and Haskell he
Was not to be found. She took herself away
To Kansas City, Kansas. Fiddle-de-dee.

Fiddle-de-dee, she said. So this is what
My mother meant. So this is what I got
For all my love and whispers. Even now
He's lying on the levee, like as not.

She had the baby and then she went to the place
She heard he might be at. She had the grace
To whisper who she was before she blew
The satisfied expression from his face.

The baby's name was Trahan. He learned to tell
How sad his daddy's death was. She cast a spell
Telling how it happened. She left out
A large part of the story but told it well.

The Muse

Driving south on U.S. 71
Forty miles from Fort Smith
I heard a woman speak from the back seat.
"You want a good idea for a closing line?"
I recognized the voice.
"Where did you come from?"
"I wiggled in back there when you stopped for gas.
You'd better pull over."
She knew about the cards I kept in my pocket
to scribble on whenever she came around.
We'd been through this before.
I bumped down from the blacktop and stopped the car.
Between a couple of oaks and a yellow line,
above the howl and sizzle of passing traffic,
she said some words. I waited. She looked out the window.
"Well?" I said. "Is that it?"
"It's all I have," she said. "Can't you do
anything for yourself?"
"I listen," I said, "That's what I'm supposed to do."
She took a slow breath and got out of the car.
"I'll try to get you something.
I'm going to walk around for a little while.
If you leave me here I'll forget I ever saw you."
"I won't leave you," I said. So I'm sitting here
between the darkening road and pin oak trees,
a 3 X 5 card in one hand, a pen in the other,
beginning to feel vulnerable and foolish
like a man waiting for more toilet paper
thinking he may have been left there and forgotten.

The Firebreathers at the
Café Deux Magots

We sit at a sidewalk table.
Noilly Prat over ice.

A firebreather lost out of time,
his cheeks full of shadows,
takes off his shirt,
starts to spin it like a bullfighter's cape
and drops it.
He opens a blue plastic bottle,
soaks a torch, a broomstick wrapped in rags,
and waves the fire in front of him like a flag.

He seems to drink the alcohol like water.
He breathes in slowly.
He exhales a burning breath
red with yellow borders.

Flames run like liquid.
They drop in brief blazes from chin to chest.

With uncooperative hands and locked-in legs
he does this for nine silent minutes.
He bows like Pinocchio to the proper applause.
Aggressively among us he collects his coins.
His eyes when they come close
are bleary and small.
He seems to be drunk.
His hair is seared away.
His eyes don't have any lashes.
Blisters have shrunk into scars
on his chest and chin
like some exotic fruit left in the field.

One eye seems to be hunting
for something on its own.

He puts the plastic bottle
the torch and the cash
into a canvas bag and wanders away.
His feet sound like gravel poured on the pavement.

A woman plays a flute.
Her tall companion
long breasts moving like lovers
inside her blouse
comes and demands our money with great hands.

Another man,
years younger,
his green eyes lifting like fingers
the faces of women,
sheds his open shirt.

His chest is perfect and hard
and clean as marble.

Over the left nipple
one small round scar.

He opens the plastic bottle. He grins.
He tosses back the hair falling into his eyes
and then he makes a small move with his head,
a small, unconscious move,
the way one turns for a moment in mid-sentence
hearing a tumbler break in another room.

Lost in Ladispoli

for Ruth

Though we may never be seen alive again
by anyone who speaks English well
surely we are somewhere in Italy still
surely we are near the Mediterranean coast moving
by some definition
in this street-wise but halfhearted collapsible Fiat
through rutted mud between these narrow houses.

What the hell way is west?
They'll find us rusted shut, down a dead-end alley,
sitting up and obviously screaming at the end
like the people of Pompeii.

When suddenly here on a building
made from this mud
on a low flat roof a girl
Who knows with these Italians?
seventeen
tall in the warm morning sun in a blue bikini so brief
it barely repeats her mouth, her low-lidded eyes,
brushing out the long, the luminous hair.

She is more Roman this girl than all of Rome.

Her body turns as if the world were turning
(Sweet Love, how like you this?)
slowly as the Fiat fumbles
churning the mud.

She raises an arm.
She may be stretching loose from the last threads of sleep.
She seems to be pointing to something.

We take the lane she shows us or seems to show us.

She gazes at us moving toward the sea
as if she has seen something remarkable
something that ought to be precisely remembered.
We stop and look back.
We gather her in
against the pull of gravity
and time
because
she has not yet heard
of either one.

In a Gradually Moving Car
Somewhere in Calcutta

The people filling the street
slide past the fenders of the car
and close in behind us,
eyes at the windows paying no attention
as if we were chugging along in a motor launch
up a river clogged with floating bodies.

No danger here, the driver says. No danger.

Rickshaw drivers don't have any shadows.
The sun falls through them onto the broken pavement.

A dog with no skin stands with stiff legs and trembles.

A woman washing her hair in the running gutter
raises her head for something that floats by.

A bride sits hard in the back of a black Buick
between solemn men like brothers.
Out of a nostril hangs a string of pearls.

The honking rises
one endless syllable
hosannah.

I think of an apple.

A one-legged boy in short black pants
hops out of an alley
as if all of us were cripples
dragging our second legs.

I think of an apple.

Two men who may be students
one wearing only a shirt
one wearing only the pants that belong to the shirt
make their almost unnoticed way
across the street,
their arms moving in quick, important ways.

The later babies, they take a hand or foot.
The driver tells me this. They beg better.
I know the driver is telling me driver's lies.
I pretend to believe him.
I frown, I shake my head.

Gray rags around her bones
a little girl crying
begins to balance her way along a rope
four feet above a clot of uncertain faces.
A woman
moves among the hands
collecting coins.

Barely above the heads
a dead man is borne on a board
riding the high hands of seven men.
He seems to be a narrow raft
down the same thick river.

I think of a single apple, dark,
with pale yellow markings around the stem,
resting in the middle of a small, round, walnut table.
A slender woman wearing a white dress,
touching the table lightly
with her long left hand
stands still and looks at the apple.
There is not a sound
except for one white curtain barely moved by the wind.

Normandy Beach

The waves on the Normandy coast jump heavily toward us.
Somewhere above the rolling, ocean-thick air
soldiers are lining up in a rising light.
The name we have come to find is whitely there.

We stand awhile above the ragged beach
where the German gunnery crews held hard
and spread the beach with bodies that still sprawl,
appearing and disappearing. A silent charge

comes out of the lifting fog, vague visions of men,
some of them drowning, some digging holes in the sand,
some lying on the sand with waves washing their boots.
We watch as the bodies fade away in the sun.

We find his name, Lieutenant, Arkansas.
To leave you there alone I turn around
to a curving monument, The Spirit of Youth
Rising Out of the Sea, what might be found

as frontispiece in a book of Romantic verse.
It must have suggested solace to someone:
arms that might be wings, and flowering waves,
what Shelley as a sculptor might have done.

I watch the statue standing over the stones
and think of what the living do to the dead.
Then suddenly what you came to do is done.
We stop in a dark store for cheese and bread

and a bottle of wine. We find that famous room
where tapestry runs like a frozen picture show
the slow invasion that went the other way
over eleven hundred years ago,

princes and knights and horses in feathers and metal
changing the names of things. An iron cross
leans from an iron gate at the foot of a hill
where careful Germans step out of a touring bus.

I don't want to make a bad metaphor here
and everything is suddenly metaphor.
We head the Fiat south in a sundown light
and follow the back roads. Beside a river

we make the wine outlast the food and sit still
and watch the water run. Thought after thought
comes into my head and goes. Lonely companion,
there's something I have to tell you but I don't know what.

Aesthetic Distance

The moon is dark. We have our drinks on a terrace
on Gianicolo hill. There is a little war
in the streets of Rome. We see the flashes from pistols,
the sweeping lights, we hear the pistols popping.
We watch a Molotov cocktail burning its curve.
"Star bright," somebody says. "Make a wish."

For Victor Jara

Mutilated and Murdered
The Soccer Stadium
Santiago, Chile

This is to say we remember. Not that remembering saves us.
Not that remembering brings anything usable back.

This is to say that we never have understood how to say this.
Out of our long unbelief what do we say to belief?

Nobody wants you to be there asking the question you ask us.
There had been others before, people who stayed to the end:

Utah and Boston and Memphis, Newgate, Geneva, Morelos—
Changing the sounds of those names, they have embarrassed us,
    too.

What shall we do with the stillness, do with the hate and the pity?
What shall we do with the love? What shall we do with the grief?

Such are the things that we think of, far from the thought that you
    hung there,
Silver inside of our heads, golden inside of our heads:

Would we have stayed to an end or would we have folded our
    faces?
Awful and awful. Good Friend. You have embarrassed our hearts.

Wiedersehen

When open trucks with German prisoners in them
passed in convoy through the small town
I dreamed in, my fourteenth year, of touchable breasts
and cars and the Cards and the Browns, we grabbed the shirts
we twisted and tied for bases and chased the trucks
past all our houses slow as we could run.

We tossed the baseball up to one of the guards
who sometimes pretended to keep it but threw it back.
Once I threw it badly. A German caught it.
A boy barely older than I was and blonder
and nearly as thin. He grinned and I thought how much
the baseball belonging to John Oscar Carpenter
must have cost. The guard didn't seem concerned
about the baseball or me. We ran for blocks
behind the flatbed truck. The side rails rattling
made the same sense the Germans did
calling and tossing the ball to one another.

We ran in silence needing our breath to breathe
and knowing that begging raises the value of things.
At the edge of town the convoy speeded up.
Everyone stopped but me and the truck pulled away.
I looked back once to see the seven others
standing on the curb of the last street
loose and surprised as a group on a picnic
looking into a river where someone has drowned.

When I turned back to the trucks, pumping my arms,
the pain in my side coming to punish me hard,
to burn the blame away and make us even,
even John Oscar Carpenter and I,
the young German hauled back and let the ball
fly in a flat arc from center field.
I caught it. I held it in the hand I waved
as truck by truck the convoy shifted gears.
"Wiedersehen," he yelled. A word I knew.
I turned and pegged the ball to home in time.
I wondered if he had killed the Rogers boy
or thrown the hand grenade at Luther Tackett
that blew his arm away. I had done something
nobody ever had done. It was large and frightful.
We walked in amazement awhile and went to our houses.

Your grandchildren, German, do they believe the story,
the boy in Arkansas, blonder than you?

We

We are pleased to present for your listening pleasure. . . .
This is Civil Defense for your own good.
Stay in your houses. This is not a test.
Something is moving barely above the trees
at the edge of the city coming in from the south.
Stay away from the windows. Turn off all lights.
If you have been caught in your car pull over and stop.
Tons of darkness are falling out of its eyes.
From every hole something resembling something
dribbles down. It glistens on the grass.
It has a certain cast. It smells like something.
It's one of ours, it's one of ours. It's all right. . . .
the Second Piano Concerto in B flat.

A Newspaper Picture of Spectators
at a Hotel Fire

At three in the afternoon on a clear day
fire breaks out in a tall St. Louis hotel
on the 16th floor and takes it from end to end.

That is how high above this street of faces
as fixed as stones three women stood in windows
with cracking glass behind them till one by one
they tested the air like swimmers and stepped stiffly out.
They come down with zeroes in their mouths.

One among the watchers has turned his back
on such important people who step into nothing,
who kick their way to the curb, to the tops of cars.
He takes away what he wants, the negative faces.

All morning we are moody. We mention the picture,
the long, slow arms, the women falling toward us.

The Story

In a small town in the mountains they tell of a man
who started showing up in pictures of weddings,
of softball teams and picnics, a dozen years
after he was sealed and weighted down
by a quarter-ton of dry mountain dirt.
His friends were Christian people full of faith.
Some took his face at first as an omen of evil,
some as a sign of favor. When nothing happened
of any special sort in a couple of years
it came to be seen as more a rude intrusion,
something they had to learn to live with
like the smell of the paper mill.
                          It was commonly held
that he was haunting the town for private reasons.
Not knowing where those reasons were likely to take him,
some people started undressing in the dark.
Twice the town council in something like secret
hired men who said they could make him go away.

One built a fire and burned hair from the barber shop.
One threw the preacher's cat off the Baptist church.
When pictures of these events came out in the paper,
the dead man was there in the crowd, watching with wide eyes.

Then one day in a shot of a prize hog
at the county fair, five years from the first appearance,
he wasn't there. Some said the burning hair
had worked exceeding slow; some said, the prayers;
some said the cries of the cat had finally done it.

Lovers began to look at each other again;
women took their magazines back to the bathroom.
People wondered what made him go away
as much as they wondered once what brought him back.

The only people who did not seem concerned
were Mary Sue Tattersall and her husband Edward
who ran the seed store at the edge of town,
kept two cows and some chickens, went to bed early,
and Saturday mornings took long walks in the woods.

Documenting It

First he could not remember
where T. S. Eliot said
"Between the plan and the act falls the shadow"
or if what he said was plan or something else.
This bothered him so that he thought of cutting back
to one or two martinis after supper.

Second he forgot
why he had driven down to the grocery store.
He sat in the parking lot for ten minutes.
Why did I drive down to the grocery store?
He went home and fixed himself a drink
and waited for his wife to ask where the soap was.

Third he could not remember
what class he was teaching,
Comparative Physiology, Biology I,
or something he had forgotten how to do.
He thought of those dreams of final examinations
in classes he registered for but never attended,
meant to but never did, couldn't find out
where it was meeting until the day of finals.
He had to go and look at the awful questions.

He found that when he panicked he was aroused.

He prayed but it did not help. It doesn't always.

Running into Things

for twelve in their pickup trucks

As lemmings run into the sea, old priests appear
at the house of Thomas Aquinas and Thomas More
to fix their faith and Hume opens the door.
They ran that way before the sea was there.

Because they couldn't remember the bypass
that cut across their roads and cut them down
a dozen farmers have died coming to town.
All they remembered was dust, gravel, and grass.

Rock

For two days I have dug around a rock
that may have been buried where it was
to hold the county in place.

I am building in front of my house
a wall of fieldstones.

Every two hours I say
I have earned a beer.

All of this afternoon
I have rolled this barely
round and enormous rock
up a gradual hill
to a place prepared
in my lonely and useless wall.

Four times the rock has pulled away
out of the crying grip of my arms and knees
and rolled back to the hole it lay in forever.

I know enough to know when to feel important.

I try to give my mind to something else.
I imagine I may be forgiven for living in town
with two dogs that don't know how to hunt
because this hurts like manhood and my hand is bleeding.

I stop and look at the blood.

I try to give my mind to something else.

It's you and I against the world my love.
The world is
I have to tell you
a prohibitive favorite.

Up there is a fence with a hole the size of this stone.
Here is a house where I live with a better woman
than I had meant to be with and two dumb dogs.

I have earned more beers than I can drink.

The woman across the street
will be naked tonight
stepping out of the bathtub
reaching for something.

My knees are gone.

It's getting late she says.
You ought to come in.

I guess I should I say but look at the rock.

It really is big she says. I don't see how you did it.

Sisyphus my friend
what does forever mean?

I go into the house. She hands me a mug of beer.

Here, unlike forever, it is six o'clock.
The big hand and the little hand, they tell us.

Trying

The husband and wife had planned it for a long time.
The message was folded into a paper boat.
The children were all asleep. In the backyard
they put the boat in the pool. *We are here. Save us.*

Rebecca at Play

She lies in the grass and spreads her golden hair
across the grass, as if in simple joy
at being what she is, quietly aware
that she is not a tree or horse or boy.

Logos

This is not the place I would like to start
but this is where I am.
Here are hats and horns and the names of states on sticks.
The speaker is spreading out the syllables
of blessings, curses, lies and incantations.
Only the lies are what they pretend to be.

Some words, put to such a use, fare badly.
They change colors. They take on mutant shapes.
They come like a pestilence flapping around the room.
Silently, one by one, they fall to the floor.
One with a tentacle, vermilion and mottled with yellow,
tries to attract my attention. I ignore it to death.

Words when they fall are like the falling of angels.
Words when they die are like the burning of feathers.
They peep like bats.

In the beginning that unbroken breath
the endless exhalation
was broken by the terrible mercy
of God's own tongue, God's teeth,
into one round verb.
Its offspring number so many
nobody could count them.

Words are shadows, words are only shadows.
We take them for more than shadows. They seem to be more.
They enlist in the armies of our poems.
They quiet unhappy lovers and name our children.
They join all things together and put them asunder.
They never hear themselves. They have no ears.
People send them out with clear directions,
Mean this, Mean that.
They undo whatever they do as soon as they do it.
A person would think we might have had enough.
Hush.

I press the silver box I have in my hand.

A jazz quintet is reinventing music.
They play with calm and perfect concentration.
There are no presidents or words in the world.
My floor is as clean as Eden.
As if by a word of God,

Let there not be words,
Let there be a magnificent moving of fingers,
Let there be reeds and brass,
Let there be piano, bass and drum.
Da-biddely-biddely-biddely-biddely-
Bump.

Ah, but we know, don't we?
A waiter can hear you make that sound all day
and he never will bring you a cheese sandwich
no matter how badly you want one.

In the beginning was F sharp.

That would have been a very different story.

People

When people are born
we lift them like little heroes
as if what they have done
is a thing to be proud of.

When people die
we cover their faces
as if dying were something
to be ashamed of.

Of shameful and varied heroic things we do
except for the starting and stopping
we are never convinced
of how we feel.
We say oh, and well.

Ah, but in the beginning
and in the end.

Paying Some Slight Attention to His Birthday the Associate Professor Goes About His Business Considering What He Sees and a Kind of Praise

Standing in front of my students,
a careful man,
I hear one tumbler turn.

The students are sitting still in their one-armed chairs
like rows of slot machines,
most surely come to rest
on the wrong combinations.

I have not helped them very much.

I love them. I tell them the truth:

The underside of the soul is rough to the touch.

The smell of the armpits of angels
is like the sound of tomatoes,
the falling of pickles.

It's easier to find the smallest needle
than prove there's not one hidden in the haystack.

For a sonnet you put two limericks together
and one verse of The Old Rugged Cross.

Now it is suppertime. I have done my job.

The sun coming down makes me feel sad and contented,
like finding the house of your life ten years ago,
another car in the driveway,
the crepe myrtle gone.

A dog drops at my feet again and again
a rubber ball to be thrown across the grass.

All of my children have loved me
more than they might have
and in their own skins do love me still.

Across the road a cow
settles into the grass
or the sun
settles into the grass like a casual cow,
slow and heavy and full to its simple face
with the unquestionable rightness of being a cow
or the sun
whichever it is going down into the grass
this suddenly silent hour, this year come round.

In Nashville, Standing in the Wooden Circle
Sawed Out from the Old Ryman Stage, the Picker
Has a Vision

for Tom T.

I'll tell you what it was. I thought about those
who suddenly came on lines they couldn't cross over—
Hank and Patsy and Hawkshaw and Gentleman Jim
and all the others who did what they did and are gone.
John Keats and Wilfred Owen and Jimmie Rodgers.

Standing a misplaced man in that crowded space
with nobody breathing but me, I had nothing to say.
My head was full of words from those good pickers
about our lives and the lives they take us to.
Lord, the years of wine and city lights.

I thought of the small square of the planet earth
I say I own, of my ridiculous self
pacing it off drunk at four in the morning
trying to understand what a place is worth.

It's a long time gone that we stopped counting things;
neither of us is going to die young.
Still fish grow fat, they lay their eternal eggs,
full grow the breasts and long the slender legs
of the young women we watch and forget about.

I heard it said by a woman in full sun
who only tells her lies from dusk till dawn
that nothing guards heaven or hell; it's the days to come
in this plain world without us we can't get through to.

I tell you, Tom, they will not let us pass.
Madness, Old Age and Death, the rough boys
who come down from the hills on bony mules
know where we mean to go and they mean to stop us.
They make a line in the dirt and stand there.
Madness we can deal with. We know his moves.
And Death's a sissy; he never comes full face
when he's all by himself. He sneaks about. He hides.
Old Age is slow but he never stops to rest.
He can chase us down like a schoolyard bully
and sit on our chests until we barely breathe
while Death creeps close to put out his fist and hit us.

So what do we do, Tom? I'll tell you what.
We take our breaths and loves to let them go
and tell the names of things to the forgetful air.

Sir

(One of the President's people has something to say
January 20, 1981)

In the first world we know there is only the present.
Nothing was or will be. Then only the future.
Then only the past, and then we are the past,

This we understand is the nature of things.

Still, when Time falls in to fill the places
our unaccountable hands have hollowed out,
we, being who we are, will flail against it
because we have not done what we meant to do,
because there has not been much that we understood
and the little we learned returned us to where we started.

This may also be in the nature of things.

We have dreamed of honor and the forthright heart
as persons blind from birth imagine light,
have barely begun to find the uses of love,
have learned to speak of that giving and greedy god
who is the earth and will not forgive us always,
into whose mouths we have lowered our fathers and mothers
and children forever. He is jealous and knows our names.

History stands, like a sad teacher, beside us,
waiting to lay a ruler across our backs
to say again that we have answered wrongly.

What we wanted to do we have not done
but we have done a hard thing to do.
Love (this most worn word) we have not understood;
on rare days, even so, we have used it well.

What we wanted to do we have not done
but we have done the longest thing to do.

This is not to commemorate an end.

What have we done? Sir, we have done right.
Right once done, there is no ending to it.

Some Lines Finished Just Before Dawn
at the Bedside of a Dying Student
It Has Snowed All Night

The blind from birth, they do not know
that roads diminish as they go
away from us. They know that in
our later years the hair grows thin.
They know it sometimes goes away.
They do not know it turns to gray.
They do not know what mirrors are.
They do not comprehend the dark
any better than the light.
They may recognize the night
as chill and a change in how things sound
and how we gather inside the house.
They do not know the way they cast
their morning shadows toward the west.
They have to trust that moon and star
are something as we say they are.
They cannot know with certainty,
whatever we say, that we can see.

Some physicists believe in four
planes of space. This is more
than we can know, lacking the sense
to see the plane our reason bends
about the other three. This
is not called faith. That's what it is.

Confessing faith, had we as well
let in God and heaven? And hell,
fastened as it is to heaven?
So the soul becomes a given,
given heaven and hell and Him?
And cherubim and seraphim?
Ghosts and ogres? Vampires? Elves?
People who can turn themselves
to cats and make potatoes rot
and curdle a mother's milk? Why not?

This man with tubes is going to die
today, tonight, tomorrow. I,
I, I, I . . . How good
that sounds to me. If I could

would I take his place? I don't
have to answer and I won't.
But I am angry at the snow
caught in the car lights. We don't know,
though we watch him, what he will do,
don't know if he is passing through
a wall or running into one,
to fall together, all of him done.

In either case we say goodbye
mostly with our eyes and try
to be exactly here, to watch
beside him while he dies, with such
an ease it seems we mean to go
beside him all the way. And so
we do. As far as we can see.
That says less than it seems to say.
Already the light when I turn that way
is dim. Sometimes I see the shapes
of people flying. Or clouds, perhaps.
Or trees. Or houses. Or nothing at all.

These are the thin thoughts you call
to the front of my mind. It's a feathery three
o'clock in the morning. We've gotten through
almost another measured night.

There's love to serve and sufficient light
in the living mode. I wish you would stay.

The nurse will disturb you soon. I will say
good morning again. I will mention the snow.
I will lie about this. I will get my coat
and tie my shoes. I will stop and stand
by the bed awhile and hold your hand
longer than you like for me to
and drive home dying more slowly than you.

In Another Town

Out of a sealed window
in a bookless room where I have stayed too long
I see a man and a woman standing on a bridge.
I wonder why they are there this hour of the morning.
They grip the railing.
I suppose they are trying to solve a problem.
They leave without touching and walk in different directions.
Daylight takes over the bridge cable by cable.
If someone were to come now and knock on the door
I would say, "Look how sunlight collects on the bridge."

Living on the Surface

The dolphin
walked upon the land a little while
and crawled back to the sea
saying something thereby
about all that we live with.

Some of us
have followed him from time to time.
Most of us stay.
Not that we know what we're doing here.

We do it anyway
lugging a small part of the sea around.
It leaks out our eyes.

We swim inside ourselves
but we walk on the land.

What's wrong, we say, what's wrong?

Think how sadness soaks into
the beds we lie on.

Jesus, we've only just got here.
We try to do what's right
but what do we know?

One Day a Woman

One day a woman picking peaches in Georgia
lost her hold on the earth and began to rise.
She grabbed limbs but leaves stripped off in her hands.
Some children saw her before she disappeared
into the white cloud, her limbs thrashing.
The children were disbelieved. The disappearance
was filed away with those of other women
who fell into bad hands and were soon forgotten.
Six months later a half-naked man in Kansas
working on the roof of the Methodist church
was seen by half a dozen well-known
and highly respected citizens to move
directly upward, his tarbrush waving,
until he shrank away to a point and vanished.
Nobody who knew about the first event
knew of the second, so no connection was made.
The tarbrush fell to earth somewhere in Missouri
unnoticed among a herd of Guernsey cows.

One of Those Rare Occurrences on a City Bus

For exactly sixty seconds riding to work
approaching a traffic light going to green
he understands everything. I mean from the outer
curling edge of the universe to quarks,
the white geometries of time, of language,
death and God, the potted plants of love.
He sits there and looks at the truth. He laughs.
What could we want, except for him to laugh?
Understanding all, he understands
he has only sixty seconds, then he returns
to live with us in ignorance again,
and little enough to laugh at. "Do you have a pen,"
he says to the man beside him,
"that I could use?" The man pats his pockets
and shakes his head and shows his open palms
to say that he is sorry. Fifty-three. Fifty-four.

Mecanic on Duty at All Times

The license plate was another state and year.
The man's slow hands, as if they had no part
in whatever happened here, followed the hollows
and hills of his broad belt. Inside the car
four children, his face again, with eyes like washers,
were as still as the woman, two fingers touching her cheek.
"How much?" he said. "Well maybe fifty dollars
if I can find a used one. I guess I can."
The hands paid no attention. Out in the sun
light wires dipped and rose and dipped again
until they disappeared. *Flats fixed* and *Gas*
and *Quaker State* squeaked in the wind. Just that.
And the speeding trucks, wailing through their tires.

WW I

Even tomorrow he may leave his room
to get the *Times* out of the holly bush
and there before him see a battleground:
trenches, the mud, the rats, the bombs that bloom
so small a man could die alone in one,
Mademoiselle from Armenteers, the sound
of tiny planes made of canvas and tin.
He may look at his watch or check the sun;
he may wait for orders to move on out,
or once more get the *Times* and take it in.

Divorce

A man existed for seventeen spidery years
in the crawl space under the rafters of his home.

His Ford was found on a bridge.
His wife stood on the slick riverbank
shifting from foot to foot
as if she had gone there with the wrong congregation.

That was when he slipped into the house.

He came down by night and took some food.
Only enough so nobody would notice.

In two or three years he learned to tell by sound
like a blind man what happened in the rooms beneath him.

He heard the children grow up as the music changed.
The girl was a Brownie Scout for a little while
and then the phone began to ring all day.
The boy let the screendoor slam till he graduated.

Sometimes his wife would bring a man home.
He understood everything,
the shutting of the door,
the stumbling in the dark,
the quietness that occupied the house.

After a Brubeck Concert

Six hundred years ago, more or less,
something more than eight million couples
coupled to have me here at last, at last.
Had not each fondling, fighting, or fumbling pair
conjoined at the exquisitely right time,
thirty-four million times, I would be an unborn,
one of the quiet ones who are less than air.
But I will be also, when six hundred years have passed,
one of seventeen million who made love
aiming without aiming to at one
barely imaginable, who may then be doing
something no one I know has ever done
or thought of doing, on some distant world
we did not know about when we were here.
Or maybe sitting in a room like this,
eating a cheese sandwich and drinking beer,
a small lamp not quite taking the room from the dark,
with someone sitting nearby, humming something
while two dogs, one far away, answer bark for bark.

Animals

I think the deaths of domestic animals
mark the sea changes in our lives.
Think how things were, when things were different.
There was an animal then, a dog or a cat,
not the one you have now, another one.
Think when things were different before that.
There was another one then. You had almost forgotten.

Jonathan Aging

Jonathan feels like a character out of Dickens.
He's served foods he can't digest anymore.
He feels things move that never have moved before.
His graying hair grows thin and his body thickens.

He thinks of mortality more than he used to.
He knows his wife has seen that his arms are soft,
that he has neither time nor interest left
to do the things she still wants to do.

He finds time for another glass of scotch
before dinner, is still surprised to hold
the paper so far away and misread his watch.

If it confuses him how people grow old
to curse the lapsing of the heart and crotch,
it was never a secret and he was certainly told.

A Poem for Emily

Small fact and fingers and farthest one from me,
a hand's width and two generations away,
in this still present I am fifty-three.
You are not yet a full day.

When I am sixty-three, when you are ten,
and you are neither closer nor as far,
your arms will fill with what you know by then,
the arithmetic and love we do and are.

When I by blood and luck am eighty-six
and you are someplace else and thirty-three
believing in sex and god and politics
with children who look not at all like me,

sometime I know you will have read them this
so they will know I love them and say so
and love their mother. Child, whatever is
is always or never was. Long ago,

a day I watched awhile beside your bed,
I wrote this down, a thing that might be kept
awhile, to tell you what I would have said
when you were who knows what and I was dead
which is I stood and loved you while you slept.

The Vanishing Point

Often I squinted my courage to see the spot
where all lines converge, but only saw
my father before it, spreading like a tree.

He is diminished now into that unplace
where there is nothing, neither breath nor breadth,
and I have felt a generation move.

I am standing, it seems all of a sudden,
with no one now between that point and me,
sliding toward it slowly as I can.

I grieve to celebrate. And may my children,
back down the widening years, see before them
some such old and serviceable simile.

On a Photograph of My Mother
at Seventeen

How come to town she was, tied bright and prim,
with not a thought of me nor much of him.

Now, tied to a chair, she tries to pull free
of it and the world. Little is left of me,

I think, or him, inside her teetering head
where we lie with the half-remembered dead.

Her bones could be as hollow as a bird's,
they are so light. Otherness of words.

They could be kite sticks. She could be a kite;
that's how thin her skin is. But now some light

from somewhere in the brain comes dimly through
then flickers and goes out. Or it seems to.

Maybe a door opened, where other men
and women come and go, and closed again.

How much we need the metaphors we make
to say and still not say, for pity's sake.

For Lucinda, Robert, and Karyn

I leave you these, good daughters and honest son,
to have or toss away
when all is said and done:

a name that rocks like a boat; some thoughts begun;
a fondness for instruments I didn't play.
I leave you these, fair daughters and far son:

a sense of the probable (the one
sure anchor for the brain); a place to stay
as long as it stands. When all is said and done

you'll share the glory I won, or might have won,
for things I said or things I meant to say.
I leave you these, tough daughters and rocky son:

a tick no springs or brain or batteries run;
the valley in the mattress where I lay.
When all is said and done,

I'll leave my unpaid debts to everyone,
a slow love and resentment's sweet decay.
I'll leave you to yourselves, my daughters, my son,
when what's to say and do has been said and done.

Staying

What are we to do with this hour of the evening
when the curving distinction between the sky and the sea
is almost gone
and the waves breaking white on the dark shore
and falling back
sound like the steady breathing of some long creature
sleeping or waiting?

In a small house high above the water
smiling for no reason I can name
you pick up a deck of cards and begin to shuffle.
We are both pleased by the riffle of the shuffling cards
which is not like any other sound.

Entropy

You say Hello and part of what you spend
to say it goes to God. There is a tax
on all our simplest thoughts and common acts.
It will come to pass that friend greets friend
and there is not a sound. Thus God subtracts
bit by little bit till in the end
there is nothing at all. Intend. Intend.

My Wife Reads the Paper at Breakfast
on the Birthday of the Scottish Poet

Poet Burns to Be Honored, the headline read.
She put it down. "They found you out," she said.

A Little Poem

for Jack Marr

We say that some are mad. In fact
if we have all the words and we
make madness mean the way they act
then they as all of us can see

are surely mad. And then again
if they have all the words and call
madness something else, well then—
well then, they are not mad at all.

One of the Crowd on the Shore Tells How It Was

Mark 5:1–17

"What a wonderful thing has come to pass,"
everyone said. It was some day, all right,
for him set free of demons, and his kin.
All of them were Christians after that.
At first the people cheered and clapped their hands.
"Jesus!" they said. "Did you see what he did?"
Except, of course, the owners of the hogs.
I can tell you they had some things to say,
with two thousand pigs running amok.
"The whole damn business gone, the years of work!
How we gonna feed our wives and kids?
Someone's gonna pay for this, by God.
Who the hell does this man think He is?"
After a while this made the crowd uneasy
and then they got to grumbling, nervouslike.
Finally they told the man to leave
but when His boat was almost out of sight
there were the owners, yelling through their hands,
"What are you going to do about our pigs?"

Love in the Cathedral

". . . except you ravish me."

In the beginning I couldn't speak to you.
Not because the words wouldn't come;
it was because they might. Not words like love,
blooming where they fall; words like come here.
When once you turned to look straight at me
out of a crowd, I thought I must have let

the sounds inside my head come out, like "let
us all go home." I wouldn't say to you
the wet, small words that moved inside of me.
I have thought that faith and patience would come
to no good end, that you would say, "See here!"
and never say, "Well yes, I think I'd love

to follow you home; to tell the truth, I'd love
to have some wine, then talk awhile, then let
you pleasure me." *Expelled to suffer here,*
John Milton wrote of us. I look at you
and in my mind your awful kinsmen come
around every corner, looking for me.

You once talked about the weather with me
and that was something, but it was not love,
did not resemble love. Love ought to come
in recognizable clothes. One day I let
my plain and earthy self talk to you
most gently, saying plainly, "Please come here,"

but everything went wrong, a bah-bah here,
a bah-bah there. You have bumped into me
by accident, I have bumped into you
on purpose on the street where talk of love
was inappropriate, then I have let
my heart hide in the cold and watched you come

laughing and blind. No matter what may come,
give me this: that all this time I stood here
ignored to death and loved you while you let
every chance go; say your glances at me
suggested almost anything but love;
say I know you cry in bed, poor you.

Believe in love. You know that I am here
to let you loose. Here is my flesh for you
who may abide with me till kingdom come.

Tearing Down the Hotel

They are tearing down the oldest hotel
in Spring Lake, New Jersey. People sat here
in wicker chairs, reading Henry James,
when women wore long dresses and high shoes
and talked to men in hard straw hats and blazers
of motorcars and Egypt. Out of their sight,
men with large hands and unbreakable words
complained to women who never slept enough.

People came here when men in medicine wagons
sold bottles of dark elixir to women who waited
in small, fictitious towns, in houses with fringes,
rocking upstairs for days, the last drop gone.

Cars and aeroplanes and moving pictures,
adventures of goggles and boots, made here once
a surety as bright as a pale wine
caught by candlelight and nearly as brief.
Then they died, but that was different, too.
They died knowing that love by vulgar love,
barring only the yawn of a God grown bored,
eternal generations would bloom above them.

When the structure someone supposes here
to take the place of this hollow hotel
is pulled apart, say in a hundred years,
someone will say, maybe, thinking of us:
they were like this and that, read such and such;
they talked of these matters in those old chairs;
they never quite believed that we would be here
recalling the dead, pulling their buildings down.

The Promotion

We are not a large concern, although compared
to what the firm was when my uncle chose
to let it run itself, we are not small.
I'm glad you both could come. Let me freshen those.
I do not mean to denigrate my uncle,
whose seed this was. No growth, not a hundredfold,
can match the making of something out of nothing.
I give him his due, but he was losing hold
when I had nothing but hold. His mind and body
both would wander. My first day, I thought
he might not outlast another clean shirt.
He would go home at noon, but still he taught
me half of what I know. I never suffered
much of an education. I lived in the hills.
I brought a small embarrassment to my uncle
and then a threat and then a battle of wills.
I knew as much as a dog does about Sunday
but I had an ease in speaking. Anyway,
you can't fall out of a well, so I took chances.
Soon my uncle was staying home all day.
I know you've heard I took this company over
by untoward means. This is purely falsehood.
It took no cunning at all—only some courage
and a sense of the differences in right and good
consistent with a changing situation.
That's a Magritte that seems to have caught your eye.
I hope I haven't bored you. Please help yourselves;
my wife made all of these. Then by and by
I had to let my young cousin go.
His father lived in the past; this one carried
the future around with him. He never believed
much in the present world. And then he married
a scarce-hipped woman. You know the kind of girl
that cooks turnips and peas in the same pot,
the kind that gets entailed in her man's affairs.
The kind of woman yours is clearly not.
You can trust a high-breasted woman.
Small women getting undressed will lay their rings
in patterns and turn their stockings right side out,
but this has no effect on the order of things.
Then there was my son, born to my first wife,
a woman with all the qualities of a hound

except loyalty. When he was grown
he smelled the bread and came scratching around.
I gave him the chance you have to give a son
even though this one, born of his mother, lied
so bad his wife had to call the dog.
I'm not at home with words. Believe I tried.
When I saw he couldn't do the job
I offered him the southwest territory.
He's somewhere selling shoes. His wife left him
with nothing but a note. That's a story
I'll tell you sometime when you care to hear it.
A man needs a woman with no disdain
for what the man is, or he has no center
and spends his time in foolishness and pain.
I need a man with pride in what he is not,
a man with simple habits I can trust,
who wants just barely more than what he's got,
who'll do me in if he can, or wait if he must.
But that's enough. My wife is giving the sign
that I must light the candles and choose the wine.
What is your pleasure?

A Summer Afternoon
An Old Man Gives Some Thought
to the Central Questions

Grass grows out of every sidewalk crack.
Briars have taken the garden.
The arteries of the old dog harden almost audibly.
The basement door is broken and the mice are back.

So this is how things are: this face
that doesn't belong to anybody,
a lot of things I ought to throw away,
the grass that knew its place.

I overdramatize somewhat. There's nothing bricks,
a hoe, some putty, nails, and luck can't fix.
Almost everything is redeemable.
The dog and I are not.

Time sometimes heals the mind
and the metaphorical heart
but ravages all the while the bones and the hair
and the poor, sad, fleshy part.

But this is something we have understood.
This was part of the deal our parents made
back in the very beginning of the dream.

I picked up a young bird yesterday
that I thought was dead.
I was going to throw it away
then one of the delicate gray lids lifted.
The eye was as large
as if a child had drawn it.
It knew me with total recognition
as a thing that would have its way.

The way a dying man
his leg in a bear trap too long
might hear either a bear or a man
coming toward him
and listen with some interest.

So it is at the end
but who would want to be an old house
who, being hammered on all day,
understood nothing?

The Aging Actress Sees Herself
a Starlet on the Late Show

For centuries only painters, poets, and sculptors
had to live with what they did as children.
Those who trod the boards—I love that—
said their first stumbling lines into air.
Some do still, but most of us who are known
and loved for being people we are not
have reels and reels of old film unrolling
behind us nearly as far as we can remember.
We drag it everywhere. How would you like
your first time doing something to keep repeating
for everyone to look at all your life?

How would you like someone who used to be you
fifty years ago coming into this room?
How would you like it, never being able
to grow old all together, to have yourself
from different times of your life, running around?

How would you like never being able
to stop moving, always to be somewhere
walking, crying, kissing, slamming a door?
You can feel it, millions of images moving;
no matter how small or disguised, you get tired.
How would you like never being able
completely, really, to die? I love that.

Schumann Adds Trombones to His Second Symphony After Mendelssohn Conducts the First Performance

I'm getting better but Mendelssohn was right.
I don't have the strength to stand there
weaving all those colors into something
no one has heard before, in front of people
who know that I went mad and suppose I am.
He was a good friend to take my place
and point the applause to me. Writing it down
took an inordinate time. Darkness fell
one quiet Sunday morning for six months.
I finished it, which ought to say something.
It hurt me not to conduct the first performance,
but there was a blessing in it. All these years
I never had a chance to stand back
and see a work the way another sees it.
Clara, it was so good I forgot it was mine.
Those long nights, lamp and candle. I got it down
almost the way I heard it. Just here and there
I think it needs a small touch of brown.

The Senator Explains a Vote

It's not my office, after all; it's yours.
I'm always pleased to see the folks I work for.
To tell the truth, I half-expected you.
I know that you're unhappy; I read your letters.

You put me on the payroll to do a job
the way you want it done; and so I do,
when I can put a name to what you want.
Sometimes the public will's so faint a thing
it's hard to find it, then I use my own.

Some tell me that I've lost the common touch
and ought to be brought home and put to work.
The fact is, being here, things do look different.
You know how the slope of a straight road
climbing a hill way off ahead of you
may look like a perpendicular rise.
You have to get close to see it right.
But you can find metaphors enough
to say you see things better from a distance.

I'm digressing. Truth is, you credit me
for more effect on history than I have.
Once I thought the sounds of what I said
would last forever, give or take a year.
I also cared a lot what others said.
You start to think, though, as you get older,
what history books will say. That question has turned
some presidents and a few supreme court
judges into decent human beings.

That's something there we ought to think about,
what we elect, electing a human being.
We've known many a grief and many a grave
and now and then a happy half an hour,
but these have not told us very much
about what we are. Talking late,
we have sometimes confessed a fear of computers,
not wanting to say that we are computers, too,
for we are slow and move at our own behest.
On the other side we keep a distance
between ourselves and the creatures. We rarely see this,
but gorillas make us nervous; even dogs do.
Between the sinless flesh and the sinless brain

we look uneasily in both directions
and hope for kind attention when we are dead.

It's hard to know, though, with what hard eyes
history may see us. We say to ourselves
that time will vindicate that one, or that one,
but who knows an hour ahead? All we can do
is make a few decisions and die with them.
History is going where it will.

But this is not what you want to know.

The fact is, the world is being invaded
and there is nothing we can do to stop it.
They will capture every government office,
they will control every church and school,
every position of power in the marketplace.
Everything we have will be theirs,
and there is no way for us to stop them
though every last one of us were Herod.
They are the children who were born last night.

One of the hardest things we have to do
is face the awful fact of the ordinary.
The world is dying. Long live the world.
I see you think I am not addressing the question.

While we browse through the evening paper
the streptococcus spawns generations,
but trees, if they could see us, would see us move
so fast we might be invisible.
We measure time by how much time we take.
Perhaps we should be still for a little while
and let things pass. But that isn't in us.

Anyway, if you can't cast a few
votes of your own, why come here at all,
a place full of people you don't like,
except to get your name in the almanac—
which, I may as well admit, is something.
My mother would have loved to see it there.

Why am I telling you this? I'm very sorry;
the bell you hear means I have a roll call.
Has anyone offered you coffee? Please keep the cups.
They have the insignia of the senate on them.

In Extremis *in Hardy, Arkansas*

My client is a scoundrel and a thief,
the prosecutor says. While he was not
arrested for a scoundrel, I admit it.
Now he says he is a liar, too.
Using the language in the strictest sense
a rhetorician, yes, would said he lied,
but what he said he said in self-defense,
and after the fact, long after the fact.
I mean, when he was captured, he denied
he was a thief. But can a man be blamed
for letting the justice system do its job
without his crying, "Warm, cool, warm"?
The point is this: before no onerous act
did this man say, "Moth may corrupt, and rust,
but I will not break in." He never claimed
to be the sort of man that you could trust.
He lied not to get, but to get away.

If you are a Jew or a Moslem, you have to say
of course you want to take the eyes and teeth.
We know the hard laws of Abraham
our cousins live by, being out of grace.
But all of us have sinned and fallen short.

You must forgive me. That was out of place.
My head apologizes for my heart.
There are no pulpits in this country's courts
and that is meet and right. So mote it be.

A legend, then, for we can learn from legends:
People once believed a wound would get well
if one could have the blade that made the wound
be blest and polished and put to holy use;
and would, conversely, start to run and smell
if that blade were buried in corruption.
No soldier after battle cleaned his sword,
but stuck it in the dung of cows and pigs.
They might have used the cesspool of a prison
the prosecutor means to send this man to
and so ensure the festering of our wounds.

If you say, as I have watched you say,
my client is hopeless, lost among the lost,
you put yourselves in peril. That is despair.

God knows what made the sad man you see,
but I will not insult you with sentiment.
I may only say, to make a point,
how being scorned and scorning come together
like two ends of a tunnel. Go in at one,
sooner or later you come out at the other.

Patient friends, this man has fallen short.
If that were all that you were charged to know,
we could have gone home long ago.
The prosecutor, who had an easy task
compared to mine, the truth being with him,
has left no doubt of it, and little to ask
of you but mercy. All of us can see
my client is a scoundrel and a thief.
Ah, but my friends, you would let him go free
if you could know the man he meant to be.

On a Trailways Bus a Man
Who Holds His Head Strangely
Speaks to the Seat Beside Him

I brought a book to make the time pass.
It's nothing but another boring thriller.
The people in it, they don't like it either.
We're going to change the whole thing around.
You ought to read it when we get it done.

It's hard to be in a book, living a life
somebody else made up, doing things
you don't like to do, starting your life
halfway through a meal, or driving to work.
Also sometimes the print is very small.

So, anyway, if the girl across the aisle
should brush her hair back, like this, or smile
in such a way as says she wants attention,
I wish that you would trade places with her.
I have more attention than most people.

I can give her any amount she wants.
Not that it will change much for me.
I've got the only future I'm going to have.
But bless me, Lord, I could have been born
somewhere else where no one speaks English.

There are places that even those that live there
never heard of, places with dictators
that force democracy on everybody
and people are poor and dumb and ride donkeys.
Lord love us all, we don't know what we do.

I needed so much to do something well
after yesterday and the day before,
I thanked a woman twice and kissed her hand
because she said I was a perfect stranger.
People have loved and left and no one remembers.

The window here could be a clock, Lord love us,
the way the fields fly by. Sometimes I pray
to be here for whatever happens next
and hope that if it's good it happens twice
or lasts a long time.

Ruby Tells All

When I was told, as Delta children were,
that crops don't grow unless you sweat at night,
I thought that it was my own sweat they meant.
I have never felt as important again
as on those early mornings, waking up,
my body slick, the moon full on the fields.
That was before air conditioning.
Farm girls sleep cool now and wake up dry
but still the cotton overflows the fields.
We lose everything that's grand and foolish;
it all becomes something else. One by one,
butterflies turn into caterpillars
and we grow up, or more or less we do,
and, Lord, we do lie then. We lie so much
truth has a false ring and it's hard to tell.

I wouldn't take crap off anybody
if I just knew that I was getting crap
in time not to take it. I could have won
a small one now and then if I was smarter,
but I've poured coffee here too many years
for men who rolled in in Peterbilts,
and I have gotten into bed with some
if they could talk and seemed to be in pain.

I never asked for anything myself;
giving is more blessed and leaves you free.
There was a man, married and fond of whiskey.
Given the limitations of men, he loved me.
Lord, we laid concern upon our bodies
but then he left. Everything has its time.
We used to dance. He made me feel the way
a human wants to feel and fears to.
He was a slow man and didn't expect.
I would get off work and find him waiting.
We'd have a drink or two and kiss awhile.
Then a bird-loud morning late one April
we woke up naked. We had made a child.
She's grown up now and gone though God knows where.
She ought to write, for I do love her dearly
who raised her carefully and dressed her well.

Everything has its time. For thirty years
I never had a thought about time.
Now, turning through newspapers, I pause
to see if anyone who passed away
was younger than I am. If one was
I feel hollow for a little while
but then it passes. Nothing matters enough
to stay bent down about. You have to see
that some things matter slightly and some don't.
Dying matters a little. So does pain.
So does being old. Men do not.
Men live by negatives, like don't give up,
don't be a coward, don't call me a liar,
don't ever tell me don't. If I could live
two hundred years and had to be a man
I'd take my grave. What's a man but a match,
a little stick to start a fire with?

My daughter knows this, if she's alive.
What could I tell her now, to bring her close,
something she doesn't know, if we met somewhere?
Maybe that I think about her father,
maybe that my fingers hurt at night,
maybe that against appearances
there is love, constancy, and kindness,
that I have dresses I have never worn.

After the Revolution for Jesus
a Secular Man Prepares
His Final Remarks

What the blind lost when radio
gave way to TV,
what the deaf lost when movies
stopped spelling out words and spoke,
was a way back in. Always, this desire
to be inside again, when the doors are closed.

On the other side of the doors
our friends and parents and grandparents
work and eat and read books and make sense and love.

The thought of being disconnected
from history or place can empty the heart;
we are most afraid,
whatever else we fear,
of feeling the memory go, and of exile.
And death, which is both at once.

Still, as our lives
are the inhalations and exhalations of gods
we ought not fear those things we know will come
and ought not hope for what we know will not.
The dogs that waited for soldiers to come home
from Philippi, New Guinea, Pennsylvania,
are all dead now whether or not the men
came back to call them.

There is no constancy but a falling away
with only love as a temporary stay
and not much assurance of that.

The desert religions are founded on sandy ways
to set ourselves free from that endless tumbling downward.
Thus we endow ourselves with gods of purpose,
the purposes of gods, and do their battles.

We are sent to war for money, but we go for God.

Prison is no place for living
but for reliving lives.
I remember a quarrel of students
proving, reproving the world;
a woman taking love

she didn't want, but needed
like a drowning swimmer
thrown a strand of barbed wire
by a kind stranger standing on the shore.

Imperfect love in that imperfect world
seemed elegant and right.
Now the old air that shaped itself to our bodies
will take the forms of others.
They will laugh with this air and pass it through their bodies
but days like ours
they will not come again to this poor planet.

I am reinventing our days together.
A man should be careful with words
at a time like this,
but lies have some attraction over the truth;
there is something in deceitful words
that sounds good to the ear.

The first layer of paint conceals the actor;
the second conceals the paint.

By which sly truth we have come to where we are.

I can hear brief choirs of rifles.
Inside my head
naked women wander toward my bed.
How gently they lie there, loving themselves to sleep.

What do we know that matters that Aeschylus did not know?

I do believe in God, the Mother and Father,
Maker of possibility, distance, and dust,
who may never come to judge or quicken the dead
but does abide. We live out our lives
inside the body of God,
a heretic and breathing universe
that feeds on the falling of sparrows
and the crumbling of nations,
the rusting away of metal
and the rotting of wood.
I will be eaten by God.
There is nothing to fear.
To die, the singers believe, is to go home.
Where should I go, going home? Lord, I am here.

The Book

I held it in my hands while he told the story.

He had found it in a fallen bunker,
a book for notes with all the pages blank.
He took it to keep for a sketchbook and diary.

He learned years later, when he showed the book
to an old bookbinder, who paled, and stepped back
a long step and told him what he held,
what he had laid the days of his life in.
It's bound, the binder said, in human skin.

I stood turning it over in my hands,
turning it in my head. Human skin.

What child did this skin fit? What man, what woman?
Dragged still full of its flesh from what dream?

Who took it off the meat? Some other one
who stayed alive by knowing how to do this?

I stared at the changing book and a horror grew,
I stared and a horror grew, which was, which is,
how beautiful it was until I knew.

Allende at the End

I've looked out from being president
and looked through power, and looked through tommyrot,
the ragged backside of government.
Not fear. Although the chance of being shot
was always there, a presence, like the ones
who stood and faced the crowds, watching for guns.

As things are I can see I might have thought
somewhat more about a violent end.
There are many bullets to be bought
when you have a world of dollars to spend.
I know they want me dead. They've paid the man.
When he can, he will, and soon he can.

It is not so very bad, though.
I have lived through winter and into spring.
You can say I went—not gladly, no,
but ready enough, considering everything,
considering it will happen anyhow,
and what Chile will come to be now.

He Glimpses a Nobler Vision

for Ed Asner

He worried every morning about the bomb,
about the ozone layer wearing away,
about the suffocation of fish in the sea.
Then watching TV one day
he heard astronomers speak of uncountable planets,
apogee and perigee,
sun beyond cooling sun through unthinkable space,
with primal soup on some and civilization
burgeoning, maybe, on every millionth one.

So he said, Vanity, vanity,
something such as we are will scurry on,
it doesn't matter where.

He thought of something like people breathing air
or something like air, and of grace.
This brought him peace for a little while,
then, thinking too long, he thought

There might not be any elephants there.

And he was back again, with all he could bear.

Thinking About Bill, Dead of AIDS

We did not know the first thing about
how blood surrenders to even the smallest threat
when old allergies turn inside out,

the body rescinding all its normal orders
to all defenders of flesh, betraying the head,
pulling its guards back from all its borders.

Thinking of friends afraid to shake your hand,
we think of your hand shaking, your mouth set,
your eyes drained of any reprimand.

Loving, we kissed you, partly to persuade
both you and us, seeing what eyes had said,
that we were loving and were not afraid.

If we had had more, we would have given more.
As it was we stood next to your bed,
stopping, though, to set our smiles at the door.

Not because we were less sure at the last.
Only because, not knowing anything yet,
we didn't know what look would hurt you least.

The Man Who Stays Up Late

He knows that when he has to go to sleep
there will be people waiting there,
standing around with unattractive patience
ready to film the picture. Every night
they shoot the same scene: a hotel room,
neon blinking on the dirty windows.
Inside the room a tall and foreign woman
is standing silently in her underwear.
She nearly smiles. With long creeping fingers
she frees it of its tender obligations.
But then they have to shoot it over again,
over and over again, until at last
the sun swelling behind her wakes him up.

Before

Before word of his painting got around
Van Gogh spent a year in a coal mine
preaching the word of God underground
to miserable men. For dragging the divine
so close to hell the church kicked him out.
This is what his paintings were all about.

Conrad earned his first living afloat.
So did Samuel Clemens. When they got
themselves settled on dry land and wrote
all of those books, they were writing what
they'd learned when they were doing what they did.
For thirty years, Charles Bukowski hid

among the horseplayers where, fast word by word
and bet by bet, he managed to survive,
while he put into shape the world he heard,
as all of us must finally contrive
to hold on to anything we've won
by making what we do from what we've done.

Geoffrey Chaucer lived with Priest and Knight,
Prioress and Nun, Pardoner and Bitch;
he also lived as Franklin. Turning to write,
he wrote about them all. What we watch
or wallow in is all that we can share.
Anything else is dreamstuff. Is air.

We bury this, though, and we let the art
rise from those graves as if it came from air.
So it is with love. When we start
to touch and wallow, sweaty, slick, and bare,
we never mention where we learned the touch
that gives such pleasure. The fact is, we're such

incredible creatures we find it hard to say
to one another, "Someone hitherto
taught me what I'll teach you how to play;
I'll show you what one showed me how to do."
But who wants *a priori*? Who invents?
In loving, new is not worth two cents

no matter the myth. We find in dusty shops,
with always three globes above the door,
half-remembered faces, sweet shapes.
For every good there was a good before.
If now there is none but us, when we undress
bless them for when they sweated against us (yes).

Missing Persons

A Neighbor Tells the Officer What He Knows

To judge by what they wore on weekdays,
he worked in, say, a factory near here;
she did what sort of thing a woman does

in matching blouse and slacks and flat heels.
Wait tables, probably, or fix hair.
They drove a pickup truck with ragged holes

where rust had eaten through, and a fender loose.
Monday through Friday at seven they rattled west.
At six they rattled home. In more or less

the time it took him to wash away the grease
they would come out again. The very worst
to say about them, across the ragged grass,

is they were beautiful. In tux and fur
they carefully uncovered a vintage Corvette, bone white,
and drove to the east. Saturday by four

they were like us again and the car was wrapped,
and they were off together to who knows what
in the old pickup truck with the seats ripped.

One day he drove the Corvette back alone,
covered it there and there he lets it sit.
He spends all weekend here and the small lawn

is growing into a wilderness of weeds.
Sometimes he hangs a gun above the seat
and heads the truck south, toward the woods.

So there you are. The only one remaining
out of two women and two men
is one silent, restless, redneck man.
But who's to say these facts have any meaning?

For Reuben, at Twelve Months

Whatever else you come to be
you will always be a year,
with numbers starting out from here
and going past where I can see,
if you are clever and cock an ear
for beast of old and boast of new,
if you are careful and keep an eye
peeled for the trolls of derring-do.
It took some luck to come this far.
That's half the game, to see how high
a number you can say you are.

The other half of you is who.
Take turns, be plain, settle for less
when less is fair, and be discreet.
Try not to waste anything.
Remember that everyone you meet
is a battlefield. If you never guess
what all the counting ought to bring
a being to, let it be done
for the harmless joy. If the world's a mess,
if we are all run into the ground,
it was good to count. The world you found
is all there is and better than none.
Sometimes it isn't bad at all,
this very like a floating ball
where marvels are many and you are one.

The Gift of Prophecy Lost

Late on Saturday morning I sat reading Hardy again
drinking a bloody mary in a cabin beside a lake
in the Missouri mountains while someone somewhere close
was playing country music. And then the print blurred.
The lyrics faded out. I blinked against a light
that filled the entire room till nothing cast a shadow
then went away as quickly. If this was spiritual
or physiological I had no way of knowing.
I only knew a sadness as if there had been something
to see in those few seconds that I had not seen.

An August Evening Outside of Nashville

Seeing a chipmunk in the yard
holding a nut between its paws
while a jay in cold regard,
in a kind of punk repose,
sheds upon it what might be
contempt, for birds in Tennessee;

Following a changing cloud
while my eyelids fill with lead;
hearing the wild bees grow loud
while a wobbling, overfed
goose scolds a lazy dog
and fungus on a rotting log

makes shapes I find a message in;
when a breeze takes the sweat
barely off my bare skin,
I can almost forget
how you were with dirty feet
all tangled in my sweaty sheet.

Rituals

I just got here myself and I feel like hell.
Yesterday I went and buried my brother.
Seven old friends helped me carry the casket
and then we went and got drunk together.
My brother killed himself. He took a dive
from ten stories up. He left his will
and wallet and pen and glasses, coins and keys,
neatly lined up on the window sill.
He didn't leave any kind of message.

O.K. We begin with the mash. It's this stuff here;
it's nothing but corn and sugar, allowed to sit
for seven days or so. It's basically beer.
I didn't invent any part of this
but I have come to think I have a way
of making it go right, a kind of touch,
not going against the grain, you might say.

My brother was a preacher. He used to stand
in front of the altar rail wiping his brow,
calling, Won't you come? Won't you come?
calling, Come tonight, come now.
He used to put me in mind of a man I saw
in front of a strip joint. He'd wave and shout,
cracking the door to show a flash of flesh,
This is the place your mother warned you about.

I surely didn't invent this. Whoever did
was dead so long ago I doubt if years
had any numbers yet to know them by.
I took it as it was told. Now it's yours.
You have to pass it along or it doesn't work.

So. You have three canisters, called in turn
cooker and thumper—you see they sit over flame—
and then the flake. Real fire. You have to burn
some kind of gas to do this indoors.
Outdoors you burn anything you've got.
The cooker holds the mash, but not too much.
When the stuff gets sufficiently hot
it passes through the aforementioned thumper
into the aforementioned flake
whence it drips out a small spigot.
It breaks at the worm—the first drip is the break,

126

the spigot's the worm—at, say, sixty proof,
at a hundred seventy-five degrees or so,
then it shoots as high as two hundred.
The drops at first will come very slow
then slowly faster. You catch it in a beaker,
then you pour it into a mason jar.
The proof begins to fall very quickly.
Every half pint it drops as far
as ten proof a jar over the whole.
A spoon of moonshine over a match will do
to test the proof. It pops into flame.
You learn to read proof in the shades of blue.
Then you can say, hell, as you sometimes will,
this ain't worth giving away, or you can say
I'm going to ask some friends to come over.
A bad year deserves a good day.

Don't get lost going back. You won't see
the signs you had for markers coming out.
They're facing the wrong way. Watch for *Baitshop
And Christian Bookstore*. Then after just about
two miles turn right. A barn roof will say
See Rock City. Jesus Christ is King.
Turn left two miles further. A rock will say
An Isolated Virtue Is A Terrible Thing.

There's not a bait and bookshop anymore.
We use the sign to give directions by.
Something like the light of a dead star.
If you've never been here before
it's still one way of knowing where you are.

The Ghost of His Wife Comes
to Tell Him How It Is

Of course you're dreaming. That's how I got here.
How else do you expect to see and hear me?
Stop trying to wake yourself. Jesus Christ!
I met him, you know. He really pays attention
to all the new people. We aren't thought of
as people, though, exactly. They call us ghosts.
No kidding. Ghosts. We don't go to heaven
until we're easy being what we are.
I'm working on that. The big problem now
is learning not to pay attention to time.

The difference is, time changes nothing.
The hell is, I still feel it passing.

A minute passes for you, and you're a minute
closer to where you're going, finally death.
In death you're never closer to anything.

What the hell are you nodding about?
You don't know a thing about forever.
Forever is full of now. That's something else
I'm still trying to get used to.

Now, for you, is three generations
with yours in the middle, all populated
by people you can see. Farther away,
we get soft and hazy like someone
seen through a screendoor at dusk.
Talking to children at breakfast or bed time,
now is three minutes or three seconds.

For me, who is nothing, not even fog,
who is only awareness without form,
now is never. Try living with that.

That's not at all what I came about.
I came to say before the last sense
of who you are fades away like a smell
in the sweet evening air, that it's all right.
Do what you have to do. Don't think about me.

I could say I love you but I don't.
Love is more substantial than I am.
Still I cared enough to come and say this.
The care was all I was, and that's it.
And who are you? And what are you doing here?

The Journalist Buys a Pig Farm

I got tired of writing the wrong stories.
Not to say there weren't interesting stories,
but we have put our minds on trivial things,
events that interest us for what they are,
and not for what they mean—planes falling,
acts of terrorism, murders, elections,
any public suffering, public power.
These sit above the fold on the front page,
while countless other moments, barely noticed,
tell us everything we need to know.

Here in the second half of the twentieth century
in a small Delta town, on a doctor's desk,
I saw three thermometers labeled in turn
oral, rectal, colored. It's not to laugh.
Or who can say if it's to laugh or not.

Late in the fourth quarter, in a vacant lot
in a small mountain town with a courthouse
surrounded by blackjack and pin oak trees
across the highway from weedy tracks
I saw on one of those rusty marquees
that get towed about from place to place,
See In Wax The Lives of Christ and Elvis.

We always say a little more than we mean.

After the two-minute warning a judge in a case
involving dancers has ruled that only nipples
and not the rest of the breast are obscene.
To laugh or not, those were the real stories.

I'm going to go raise pigs now and read
biographies and listen to old music.

A long time I tried to deal with truth
as if a truth were true for everyone.
No. It's true for those who know it's true.

I call this a truth, for one example,
that given what we are and what we do
we have to think continually of heroes
or be dragged to madness of some sort
in which we are ones, as we have dreamed, and zeroes,
however serious and of good report.

If you can say that's not true, it's not.
It's so if you know it's so. Then you can see
how nigh impossible it finally got,
how head-down hard it did come to be
putting the world to words. I tell you what.

He Speaks to His Arguing Friends and to Himself

Rattle, rattle. There is no question
except the question of final cause.
The soul, free will, the afterlife,
the dream of universal laws,
prayer, and sacrifice, and honor,
works, and faith, and greed, and lust,
might mean something or might not
depending on the source of dust.

Think of all there is as nothing,
not an atom, not a quark,
unexisting in a place,
pure unplace, not light, not dark.
Imagine that it all explodes
(although there's nothing to explode)
till matter and energy come to be.
This is one impossible road.

Imagine a mind that always was,
where *In the beginning* makes no sense.
Think it thinks us into being.
Think it knows us past our ends.
Given the mind, it came from where?
Or, free of it, we came from what?
These are the only ways to come.
Either way, you'd bet not.

But we have believed through such pain
and made such music for so long
that it would be a hurt and shame
if we should learn that we were wrong.
We have enough to fret about.
Almost all of us concur,
we'll live with the holidays we have
and the grace of God as if it were.

A Glass Darkly

for Will Campbell

At one of those bars where they weigh you at the door
so you don't fight out of your class
I took a stool away from the jukebox
and nodded toward a beer. I was slammed a glass.

The bartender looked like he'd sat on the bank all day
and still didn't have a full string.
You could look straight into his eyes
and see the back of his skull. "There's not a thing,"

I said to the man on my left, "gets cold as beer."
I asked him how he was doing. He gave me a look
to say his heart would last him the rest of his life.
"Homemade," he said, "is better." I guess it took

another two glasses to tell about
my mother, who doubted God. He gave me a glance
to say he didn't believe I told him that.
"Like all this," he said, "is stupid chance.

Ask about the planets and all the stars.
Ask about a snow goose, how it goes
to Alaska and back, not ever getting lost.
How about your finger fits your nose?

How about that woman?" You wouldn't believe
that woman waiting tables, whatever she said.
She wasn't a common truck stop beauty.
Her smile smeared the air when she turned her head.

You could make love to her with one foot in a fire.
I stared at her with total disregard.
"That's a caramel-covered ball bearing,"
he said, to say that she was secretly hard.

"When people say ritual," I said,
"they intend graduation. They don't intend
paying bills or castrating hogs
or drinking in a bar at the back end

of a stingy day." The lady wiping up
said, "Do you want another?" He said, "No'm,
I better not." Still he didn't leave.
"Where are you from," I said. He said, "Home."